The Steel-Bar Motel

The Steel-Bar Motel

Ed Fedorowich

Authors Choice Press
San Jose New York Lincoln Shanghai

The Steel-Bar Motel

Authors Choice Press
an imprint of iUniverse.com, Inc.

For information address:
iUniverse.com, Inc.
620 North 48th Street, Suite 201
Lincoln, NE 68504-3467
www.iuniverse.com

Originally published by NPI

ISBN: 0-595-13240-5

Printed in the United States of America

These are true stories about real people. The events I've described happened during the last three years of the existence of the Seyms Street Jail, in Hartford, Connecticut, where I held the position of Correctional Sergeant.

I have changed the names of all the inmates and some of the staff. This was done for confidentiality purposes as well as to save them embarrassment.

The jail is gone, as are many of the men and women who served there, but, their spirits and brave lives should always be remembered by the public that they served. This book is dedicated to the staff of the Seyms Street Jail—alive and dead.

Special Note: *All photographs were taken by the author a week after the inmates were transferred to another facility. Maintenance crews had begun to remove useful items, such as toilets, prior to the destruction of the building.*

The original entrance section to the Old Jail.

The parking lot with the East Wing in the center of the picture.

The inmate   kitchen.

The entrance to the Northwest Wing where inmates under eighteen years old were housed. The sign on the left (All Blues keep away from this area) was a warning to sentenced inmates, who wore blue uniforms, to stay away from the "kiddy wing". This wing also housed segregated inmates on the upper tiers. They were put there either for their own protection or because of a punishment sentence from the disciplinary court.

IV

The recreation area on one side of the Northwest Wing's cellblock. Also known as the "bullpen".

The East Wing's bullpen. Inmates used this area for inside recreation. This wing housed inmates who, primarily, had not yet made their first court appearance and were unable to make bond.

An East Wing cell. Whenever there was only one inmate assigned to the cell wise inmates chose the upper bunk to stay away from Ben.

VII

An East Wing walkway. The cells (right side) were open to view, unlike the front of the cells which had a solid steel door. Officers took their counts from these corridors, and inmate janitors (called "tiermen") served water in paper cups through the bars. The only running water in the cells was for the toilets.

The main corridor leading from the front entrance. The Old Jail is on the left. Staff had to walk down this aisle to get to the roll call room. If tensions were high, it was a good idea to look up for flying debris (mop buckets, plywood bed boards, etc.).

The Hole. The only ventilation was provided by the 12" fan in the far wall. The cells were directly above the furnaces. The lights went on only when the door was opened by a staff member. Five gallon pails were the only bathroom facilities.

X

New Kid on the Block

José was sixteen years old when he went to Seyms Street. He'd been arrested before, but his mother had always been there to get him out. Not this time. Either his mother was teaching him a lesson by letting him stay in jail, or she couldn't come up with his bond money.

He shuffled up the stairs to the Admittance and Processing (A&P) door, chained to other men and escorted by two police officers. When the door opened, they staggered into a five by twelve foot room. Three sides of it were made up of chain link fencing. While one of the officers removed their chains, the other presented their papers to a correctional officer (C/O).

Another C/O patted them down and ordered them to go

into a holding room. The officers seemed detached and bored. Some of the arrested men were anxious, but would never think of showing it. José was scared shitless!

He remembered the stories of the big black studs who changed boys into women. He knew that he needed to be tough and find some friends for self-defense. Even now he saw some of the older men looking him over. One said, "Hey look! Fresh meat!" He found a place on the bench, in a corner, and sat without making eye contact with anyone.

During the next hour, some men left to be processed into the jail, but the crowd in the waiting room didn't thin out. More inmates were brought in by other police departments. José tried to become invisible, especially on the three different occasions when men came over and tried to talk to him. One kept putting his hands on José's knee. All José could do was say, "Leave me alone!" and push the man's hand away.

A tray of sandwiches and milk containers was brought in, but José was afraid to get up off of his bench to grab one. He let his protesting stomach resume its growling.

After two hours, his name was called and he bolted for the door. It was opened by a C/O who chuckled, knowingly. "They give you a hard time?" he asked. José tried his best to cut him down with a look. The C/O gestured to a desk where another officer prepared to ask José a million questions for background information.

When the questioning was over, the first officer told José to strip. He hesitated as inmate workers started to gather in the area with their grinning faces. The officer who had taken down his information growled, "What the fuck are you guys staring at? You never saw a cock before? Get back to work!" They laughed and moved off. One of them said, "Hey, we were just hoping to see some pussy." Despite himself, José blushed as he took his clothes off.

The officer looked in his mouth and ears, under his arms, under his testicles, under his feet, and had him bend over to expose his rectum. This brought jeers and comments from the inmates who watched through cracks in doors and windows.

José felt totally defenseless and vulnerable. He almost cried.

José was given a towel and a little cup with liquid soap in it. He was told to use the soap on his groin area when he showered. There was one other person in the shower room, a skinny white kid. The white kid looked startled when José walked in. José thought, "Do I look that scared?" and resolved not to show his fear in the future. Neither José nor the other inmate could bring themselves to wash their faces for fear of being unable to see if another inmate entered. The officers had purposely processed these two at the same time so that nothing would happen in the shower. They held off in processing other inmates until these two were finished and dressed.

José's hair still dripped and his brown uniform smelled funny as he waited by the A&P door to be escorted to his block. A harried-looking officer finally arrived and the A&P officer told him, "Take these two to the kiddy wing."

José had only had time to tie one of his boots before the officer said, "Let's go!" His untied boot made a clomping noise that he more felt than heard over the loud music coming from the P.A. The music was so loud that it seemed to wrap him in vibration, protecting him from hearing the jeers of the older inmates who seemed to be everywhere.

They followed the officer past a control center and turned down a long hallway. On the left was a cell block that seemed to go up forever. José looked straight ahead and kept walking. They came to a dormitory that had bars separating it from the hallway and turned left. The officer stopped at a gray, steel door and knocked on the little plexiglas window with a key. When the door was opened, he stepped aside and said, "Welcome to the Northwest Wing."

An officer took their cards and turned to a small desk that was attached to a wall. As he wrote, José looked around. The cells in this block were in the middle of the building. There were bars going from the second floor walkway up to the ceiling. These would prevent any inmates who were out of their cells on the second or third level from falling to the ground. José would later learn that the two upper floors were used to house inmates who were in segregation status—the jail within a jail. These inmates were only allowed out of their cells (onto the walkway) for one hour each day. During that time they had to take a shower if they wanted one.

José looked at the area. On ground level, between the cells and the outer walls, there were picnic tables and a TV mounted on the wall. A bunch of guys his own age were playing cards or watching TV. "This might not be too bad," he thought. But, he did notice that most of them were bigger. The officer opened the chain link fence and showed them to their cells. As he followed through what he would later learn was called the "bullpen," José noticed a small shower area.

The officer unlocked his cell and left. José noticed the two bunks and the toilet bowl. The bottom bunk was made, so he put his bedding on the top bunk. As he made his bed, he realized that there wasn't a pillow. He looked around the cell and saw two pillows on the lower bunk. As he took one pillow, he heard a voice behind him say, "That's my fucking pillow." José was startled by not only the closeness of the voice, but, also, by its ferocity.

He turned and started to say, "But you have two." He only got as far as "But" when he felt a force against his chest that propelled him to the wall. He landed with a thud that sent showers of pain through his back. As José struggled for breath he sank down and ended up sitting on the toilet. A shiny black face filled his vision and he heard, "Listen good, motherfucker. You're in my house. You don't touch anything until you ask. You got that?" José weakly nodded and bent over, feeling the need to throw up. But he didn't. The inmate replaced the pillow on the bottom bunk, and walked out of the cell.

José managed to crawl up onto his bunk, and lay there trying to muffle the sounds of his sobs. After a while he curled into a fetal position and fell asleep.

He didn't hear the cell door slam, the TV go off, or the officer shout "Count time!" During the night he woke with a full bladder, but was afraid to climb down and relieve himself. He laid there, half awake and in pain, until the lights came on and he heard the shout, "Breakfast!"

During that day he met his cell partner, Jefferson, who was his height, but stockier than José.

He learned from the other inmates that Jefferson, who was seventeen, was awaiting trial for murder. The other inmates, although just as young as José, seemed to have a worldliness about them. They'd been locked up before and knew what to expect.

José noticed that four of the black inmates seemed to stay in a group by themselves. When he asked another Hispanic inmate about them, he was told that they were "trouble" and to stay away from them. The other inmate didn't tell José how he was going to do that when they lived together. José saw that Jefferson wasn't part of that group.

During the noon feeding, while the block officer was on the upper tiers helping to feed the segregation inmates, José turned from the TV program he was watching and saw the white inmate that he'd come in with stagger out of the shower area. His mouth was bleeding, his face was pale, and he was vainly trying to hold his pants up. He shuffled toward his cell, bent over and grasping at the cellbars that he passed.

José nudged the inmate next to him, and said, "What's with him?" As the inmate turned to see what José was talking about, three black inmates stepped out of the shower area, looking furtive but at the same time, smug. The inmate that José had been questioning quickly turned back to the TV and whispered, "They've just made him a woman." When he saw the confusion on José's face, he said, "They just raped him, man. Keep out of it and watch yourself. You might be next!"

Fear riveted José to his seat. He was unable to speak. Unable to move. What would he do if...?

What could he do against all of them?

José spent the rest of the afternoon pacing in the bullpen. He looked for a way out, a weapon, but found nothing that might save him. Sweat soaked his clothing and rolled off of his forehead into his eyes. It took his last ounce of strength to walk back to the confines of his cell for the afternoon count. When the door closed, he couldn't breathe. Then the disembodied voice called. "José, baby, you're next!"

I was working the four P.M. to midnight watch, that night, with Captain Bergsten. It was shortly before the last count for our shift when I went to find him to ask him a question. I was told that the captain was in the Northwest Wing, checking the segregation inmates.

I entered the Northwest Wing and asked the officer where I could find the captain. He gestured toward the upper tier, and was about to say something, when we heard the captain shout for help. I looked up and saw an inmate dangling from bars over the bullpen, three stories up.

I rushed up the stairs and found Captain Bergsten pulling on the inmate's arms through the bars, keeping him from jumping. The inmate kept shouting, "Let me go! I want to jump!" José had found what he thought was the best way out of his predicament.

The captain assured me that he could hold the inmate and sent me for handcuffs. When I returned, we handcuffed José with a bar between his arms. Now, unless he could slip out of the cuffs, he wouldn't be able to jump. The captain continued to hold his arms, and suddenly there was inmate Jefferson, on the outside of the bars, using his body to pin José so he couldn't jump. José kept screaming, "I want to die! I want to die!" Tears streamed down his face.

I sent an officer to the control center for any straps or belly-chains that he could find, and went to the boiler room to search for a ladder. We got the ladder up and I was able to strap José to the bars. Someone had notified the Medical Department because when I looked down, Medic Doug Miller was climbing up the ladder with a hypodermic syringe clasped between his teeth. I almost fell from laughing because he looked like a pirate climbing the mast.

When he got to a position just below José, Doug removed

the hypo from his teeth and said, "Pull his pants down!" José stopped screaming, looked down, and said, "I don't want a SHOTTTTT!" as Doug slid the needle into his buttocks.

José soon slumped down as the shot began to work. When I realized that we had a partially conscious person tied to the bars, three stories up, my first thought was, "What are you going to do now, stupid?" Captain Bergsten solved my dilemma by sending someone for a rope.

When the rope arrived, we looped it through the bars above José, tied it around his waist, and untied the straps that were holding him to the bars. While officers took up the slack, I put him over my shoulder, and took him to the ground.

After José was put on a suicide watch in the Medical Ward, one of the homosexual inmates approached me and said, "Sergeant, you know that I don't like most of the officers here, you included, but that was a fine thing that you people did tonight." I thanked him for his praise. Everyone likes recognition. Of course, the same inmate, a few years later, ended up stabbing me in the chest with two pencils. But that's another story.

"So You Want To Be A Sergeant?"

"So you want to be a sergeant?" Deputy Warden Gudzunas asked me. We were seated in the warden's office of the Seyms Street Jail. I thought back over my brief, three year career with the Department of Correction. I had known, early on, that I wanted to rise in rank. I remembered a captain (who'd once been my boss) telling me that if I expected to go up through the ranks, I would have to spend some time in the jails. When I was notified of this interview, I became determined to get the job. Now, as I faced the warden and deputy warden, I wasn't too sure that I was doing the right thing.

I looked around the office. It was clean and neat; but everything looked old. It seemed to have been furnished with cast-offs. This wasn't like the offices in the prisons that I had

9

worked in before. I wondered what the conditions that the officers and supervisors worked under were like if this was the best that the department could do for the warden.

As the interview progressed, Deputy Warden Gudzunas did his best to paint a factual picture for me. Expressions like: "We don't have a budget like the prisons. We have to make do," and, "You can expect to break up a lot of fights," kept cropping up in his talk. I had already seen the disaster area that surrounded the jail. Now he arranged for a tour of the inside of the facility.

Before we entered the facility, my guide showed me the Control Center. It was manned by one officer who was doing a good imitation of a squirrel gathering nuts for the winter. He ran to the glass window that faced into the jail, answered an inmate's question, hopped to the telephone that had been ringing for a while, dragged the phone to the push-button that controlled the door to let someone in, finished his telephone conversation and flew to the radio to answer someone that was calling on it. He was a blur of motion, and I turned to my guide and said, "Is it always this busy?" He seemed surprised that I'd think that this was unusual. After he pointed out the various control buttons, radio, closed circuit TV monitors, and keyboards, we entered through the first door of the "sallyport." This is a control point, comprised of two or more doors, that act to isolate the people entering and exiting the institution. The person who was between these doors was somewhat at the mercy of the officer controlling the buttons. Attorneys who wanted to visit their clients could be held there while they were identified and had their attaché cases searched.

After passing through the sallyport, we turned left and entered through another electrically controlled gate. The sign over the door said Hospital. Ahead of us was a tiny room that acted as an office and examining room. On the right was a row of cells with barred gates for doors. I looked into the first cell and was confronted by a pair of eyes with a thousand yard stare. The owner sat, unmoving on a cot. His shoulders slumped and his hands were tightly clenched together. As I watched, he began to rock back and forth. A high pitched moan escaped between clenched teeth.

The "hospital's" walls were bricks that had been painted and repainted over the years. The smell was a combination of urine, vomit, and Lysol that struck me forcefully at first, but soon was ignored by my senses. As I was shown around, depression settled on me. The closest I had come to something like this was when I'd read a description of an old insane asylum.

We left the medical area and, again, turned left. My guide knocked on a door, and we were eventually let into a large room that he called, "the A.P." This was the area where inmates were admitted and processed. They were, also, discharged, sent to court, and processed for medical trips through this room. My first impression of this area was of total chaos. Inmates were being searched, showered, and dressed in jail uniforms. There was constant movement. My opinion changed when I had a chance to observe the three officers who were assigned there. They were calm amidst the bedlam. Each went about his duties with a deliberate air that spoke of years of practice.

Months later, I was shown the basement under the AP. I stepped through the ever-present puddles and looked at the old cells that were no longer used. There were still devices attached to the walls that had been used to chain the occupants to the wall. I'm glad that my guide didn't take me there on my first tour. You could feel the presence of ghosts when you went there at night.

We walked passed the Control Center. On the right I saw small visiting rooms that were used for attorney visits. On the left was a cell block that my guide identified as the Boundover Block. It had been constructed in the middle of a large, open area within the jail. It reached from the ground to the ceiling and was three stories high. We came to an open area that held a flight of steel steps. After climbing them, we stood in front of a barred door. While we waited there, my guide yelled, "On the door!" An officer jumped up from his chair. An inmate had been shining his shoes.

As we entered the block (which I was told was called the East Wing), we were standing on a wooden-floored landing. Everything else in my view was made of concrete or steel. There was a desk that was positioned so that its occupant could look down into the recreation area. The cells were on both sides, and were four levels high. In a corner of the landing, an inmate was cutting another inmate's hair. In the recreation area, inmates were seated at picnic tables. They were playing cards or watching a large screened TV. From somewhere below, steam rose and I could hear the sounds of showers.

After being shown around the block, I followed my guide back to the Control Center. I thought my tour was completed, but he turned right at the Control Center and went down a long corridor. Ahead of us was a dormitory that was separated from the corridor by bars. On the left was a tall cellblock. Inmates were loitering on each tier, inspecting the traffic that went past. At the dormitory we turned to the right and entered the mess hall. The smell of floors washed with dirty mops was like a physical barrier that stopped us at the door. After a glance we turned and walked to a door marked Northwest Wing.

Our knock produced an immediate response from an officer who had, apparently, been sitting right next to the door. He unlocked it and ushered us in. This block was built with the cells in the center. If you were to stand by the door and look in you'd see an outside wall on the far left. As your eyes moved to the right, you'd see an open area that was used for recreation. Then would come the cells, another open area that was used for the inmates on that side of the block, and, finally, the other outside wall. This was a relatively quiet block. The first tier on each side was used to house teenage inmates. The top two tiers were used to keep inmates who had run afoul of the institution's rules. They'd gone before a Disciplinary Committee, had a hearing, and been assigned here until they could change their behavior.

When we left the Northwest Wing, we turned right, back toward the Control Center. My guide stopped at the second door on the left, and used a key to let us through a screened door. He told me that this was where the lieutenants' office, the deputy wardens' offices, and the staff mess hall were located. We sat down with a cup of coffee and he asked if there were any questions. Fearing that my questions would be reported back to the warden, I restrained myself from asking if this place was always such a madhouse. Instead, I asked about staffing levels, staff morale, and other items that would exhibit an interest in the uncontrolled insane asylum.

The interview, tour, and questions apparently worked. A few days later, I was contacted and offered the position of sergeant. My first thought, when I heard the news, was, "So you want to be a sergeant?" Or do you?

Gone Fishin'

Inmates can be very ingenious. They have little to do all day but sit and scheme. One of the examples of their inventiveness involved their version of "fishing."

The Seyms Street Jail was in the heart of Hartford's North End. This is an area that is usually described as a "ghetto," but would remind the hapless traveler of Beirut. On three sides, the jail was separated from the sidewalk by an eight-foot wall that was about twenty feet from the building. The fourth side abutted a parking lot for staff and visitors that was open to any pedestrian that wanted to make a slight detour from the sidewalk. The only outside patrols were on the two night shifts. These consisted of one or two officers walking around the jail inside the wall.

The inmates knew our shift and patrol schedules and tried to work around us. They would do this by "fishing" when no one would be expected to be checking the outside of the building or going to or from work.

During those times they would simply drop a line out a window and hope that their confederate on the street tied the expected contraband to the right line. When no one was looking, they'd reel it in.

One evening, Officer Eddie Colon was walking by an open window in the East Wing. He heard a woman's voice calling from the parking lot. "Enrique," she called. He noticed a line tied to one corner of the window, hanging down. Eddie called to her, in Spanish, "What do you want?" She said, "Give this to Enrique Sanchez." He asked, "Who shall I tell him it's from?" She replied, "He'll know. It's on the envelope."

C/O Colon reeled in the string and found an envelope containing marijuana. The envelope was addressed to the woman who was later arrested by the state police. That's why they call it "jail" not "Yale."

Crazy Louie

Crazy Louie left the alley where he'd just stabbed a drunk like himself. Louie had been sleeping, curled up next to a dumpster. His bottle of wine was his teddy bear and last week's newspapers were his blanket. Suddenly, he felt the half empty bottle being pried from his grasp. The fog over his eyes cleared slightly and he roared, "No! It's mine!" Above him stood another old drunk, sweating with the effort of fighting for the booze.

As they rolled in the slime of the alley they tried to throw punches at each other. Some of these feeble attempts actually landed on their opponent's head and shoulders, but neither was winning the fight for the bottle. The bottle slipped from their hands and began to add its contents to the grime in the alley. Louie saw it trickling away. In a rage he reached for his sock where he kept his stolen steak knife. He brought it out and drove it into his enemy's neck. Even after the blade snapped on the second thrust, he continued the stabbing motion.

Louie was crying and stabbing. Snot was running from his nose. After what seemed like a long time, he realized that his enemy wasn't moving. He looked down at him and saw all the blood. He looked at his own hands and saw that they were covered. Throwing the knife's handle away, he began to rub his hands on his pants. A thought crashed through his mind and he whirled around, trying to find his bottle. Most of the wine had leaked out, but there was still enough for a few swallows. He sank to the ground and drank.

It only took those few gulps to make him drunk again. His breathing had almost returned to normal when the last few drops spilled down his whiskered chin. He let the bottle slip from his fingers and was startled when it clinked on the pavement. Louie looked at the body and felt anger rising. By carefully pushing on the wall with both arms he was able to slowly rise to his feet. He leaned there for a moment and then staggered toward the mouth of the alley. As he passed the body, he kicked it as hard as he could, tripping in the process.

Louie walked from the alley onto the busy street. He was unaware of the pedestrians' stares as he stumbled along, muttering to himself. As he leaned against a light pole he realized that someone was prodding him and saying something. A police officer was tapping him on the shoulder, and asking if he was all right. Fear and anger seized Louie. He was trapped. Before the officer could react, Louie jumped at him. His dirty, cracked nails raked the officer's face, just missing his eyes.

Louie was booked for murder and assault. At a preliminary hearing, the judge ordered that a psychiatric evaluation be made so that Louie's fitness for trial could be determined.

The psychiatrist was seated in one of the visiting booths at Seyms Street by Officer Al Monico Sr. Then Al called the

East Wing to have Louie sent out. That evening, as often happened at Seyms Street, we were short staffed. When this occurred, the sergeant on duty would assume a post—usually the Boundover Block. That post left the sergeant with some free time to perform other functions.

As I was finishing supper a bell reverberated through the halls. This bell was the bane of everyone who pulled the Boundover Block. It meant that the control center officer wanted you to come to the Control Center for some routine task. I finished my meal and walked down the hall to see what Al wanted.

As I approached, I could see that he was upset. From a distance I saw him waving at someone who was out of my sight. He was yelling something through the cutout in the window. When I got there he said, "Go get that asshole that's over by the East Wing."

I walked to the stairway leading up to the East Wing and saw an inmate standing at the door, waiting to be let in. He saw me, and before I could speak, said, "Fuck you!" I stopped in my tracks as Officer Tom Knapp opened the door and said, "Get in here, Louie!"

I walked in to the block right after the inmate and asked Tom, "What's with this guy?" As his mouth opened to speak, the phone rang and he gestured to me to hold on for a second. Suddenly, the inmate roared, "Fuck you! I'll get out and rape your mother." He was right next to me. As his hands began to rise I grabbed him by the chest and slammed him back into the wall. Tom yelled, "Stop!" I told him to open the door as he rushed over. Then I said to the inmate, "You're going to the Hole!"

As we got to the bottom of the stairs, I said, "Keep going. Straight ahead." He wheeled around with his fingers curved like talons. As he reached for my face, I side-stepped and hit him in the stomach. This seemed to take some of the wind out of his sails because he didn't resist as I pushed him down the hall toward the lieutenants' office. When I told him to stop and reached for my key, he spun around and again tried to attack me. Luckily, there were several officers eating supper a short distance away. We were able to subdue Louie and put him in the Hole. That was another case where a lot of trouble could have been avoided if we had been allowed to carry handcuffs.

Officer Monico later contacted me and explained that Louie had come to the Control Center when called. For one reason or another he'd decided to go back to his block and wouldn't listen to Al. Then he explained that the "shrink" was still here and wanted to see Louie. I told Al, "Between you and me, he can go fuck himself." Al asked, "Is that what you want me to tell him?" I said, "Explain that his client has been put under close observation because of his violent behavior." Al said, "Then can I tell him to go fuck himself?"

Big Ben

Big Ben was a rat! Not just any rat, Ben was a jail rat. The Maintenance Department had hired exterminators who gassed, poisoned and even tried to drown Ben by hosing the drains that they suspected he traveled through. Nothing worked! After each application, he would return, and people swore he was even bigger than before.

Ben must have been pretty old. He was the size of a small cat. More than that, he looked like he had seen many rat wars. One ear had gouges and slits and his face was a mass of scars. Part of his tail was missing.

I met Ben during my first week at Seyms Street. The policy at that time was that there be a sergeant assigned to supervise the East Wing. This was the largest block in the

21

jail—four tiers high. It housed inmates who were fresh off the street and might be returning to the street after their next court appearance. Needless to say, they weren't in any hurry to comply with the orders of staff, and had to act tough to maintain their reputations.

The first night that I was assigned to the East Wing was a busy one. We were glad when lock-up time arrived and we could relax a little. The officers' desk in the East Wing was on the second tier so that staff could look down on the inmates in the bullpen during recreation. This allowed anyone at the desk to have an unobstructed view. I was sitting there, after lock-up and count-time, talking to Officer Al Plante.

I made it a personal policy, as a newly appointed supervisor, to talk with the officers as much as possible. In this way, I learned about them as well as the job that we were all suppose to be doing. I had transferred into the jail from a large prison. This was another world that required me to learn new norms of behavior.

Many of the officers who had worked in the jail a long time must have appreciated this approach because several would make it a point to try to show me the ropes. Al was one of these in his quiet, somewhat shy way.

We were talking, when I caught a movement out of the corner of my eye. I turned to see what it was, but nothing was there. Thinking that I'd become particularly paranoid that night, I went back to our conversation, but I kept watching the area where I'd seen something move. A short while later, that "something" reappeared—crawling out from under one of the cell doors. A huge rat sat up and started eating a tidbit that he held in his paws.

I said, "Holy shit! What's that?" Al's head whipped around and his eyes searched for what I had seen. Slowly, a smile of relief came to his face, "Oh, that. That's just Ben!" he said. Visions of walking a darkened tier, rounding a corner, and finding "just Ben" glaring at me with red eyes blazing flashed through my mind. I asked, "Shouldn't we do something?" Al said, "Oh, sure!" and got up and grabbed a roll of toilet paper from the desk. He stuck it and his arm through the bars and lobbed the roll at Ben. Ben didn't move. He didn't flinch. I don't think he even blinked as the toilet paper bounced near him. He looked at Al, and in rat-talk suggested that he perform an unnatural act upon himself. Then he finished the last of the morsel, licked his paws, and went into the next cell in the line.

The suburban white-boy in me asked, "Shouldn't we report it, so they can get an exterminator in to kill it before it bites someone?" Al explained that the exterminator came in regularly and had tried everything in his bag of tricks to kill Ben. Nothing worked. Some inmates and staff at various times had tried to beat him to death with sticks and clubs. "That's the only time that I know of that Ben has bitten someone," said Al.

Since he'd worked there a while, I respected Al's opinion, but, as a new supervisor, I felt that something more had to be done. In the next few days, I talked with lieutenants, captains, and, finally, the deputy warden. All greeted my concerns with the same knowing amusement that all new kids on the block are treated with, and explained the same things that I'd heard from Al. The deputy warden agreed to tell the exterminator about Ben and have him try again. To the day they tore the old jail down, Ben made his nightly rounds from cell to cell— looking for tidbits of food that inmates had sneaked into their cells. I wonder where he is now? Do he or his descendants still roam the park that is where the jail use to be?

What went through his head when he poked his nose out of the sewer and found open air where there use to be a building? I can hear him muttering in rat-talk, "The damn exterminators are at it again! They can't fool me. I know the jail is around here somewhere." Considering the ghetto that surrounded the formal jail, maybe he's right.

Knock, Knock, Who's There?

On the 4–12 shift at Seyms Street we would send an officer outside the building each night to patrol the area between the wall and the building. The officers who did this would often find drugs and other contraband that had been thrown over the wall, intended for inmates. On one night, I was standing in the hall by the officers' mess hall, talking to Lieutenant Ralph Eastman when I saw two officers go out the front door to perform this patrol. Officer Trudo was breaking in a new man, Officer Gosselin, on the outside patrol. They'd only been gone a short while when they came back in and ran to where we were standing. Both were breathing deeply from running and excitement.

They blurted out, between gasps, that as they rounded a

corner of the building by the end of the parking lot, they heard someone pounding on the wall, trying to break out. Lieutenant Eastman asked if they could see a hole or any sign of the escapees breaking through the last layer of bricks. They said that there was no sign of a hole.

The lieutenant said that from the description of the location that we'd received, the inmates had to be in the hose room at the back corner of the East Wing. The only thing we couldn't figure out was how they got into that room. They must have either had a key or been let in by a staff member. The standing order for staff was that if they let anyone in that area to clean up, an officer must stay with the crew. We feared that one or more officers had been taken captive.

Lieutenant Eastman had me call the East Wing to see if everything was all right. I spoke with Officer Jones, and without telling him what was happening, asked if he knew where all the assigned staff where at that moment.

When he said he did know, I told him to have all of them gather by the desk and that I'd be right there.

Fearing that the inmates might break through the wall at any moment, Lieutenant Eastman drew a weapon and stationed himself outside the section of building that the noise was coming from. Before he left, he told me to gather as many officers as I could, draw mace and handcuffs from the Control Center, and go after the inmates from the inside of the building.

I figured that if I entered the East Wing with a lot of officers, inmates would see us and warn the escapees. If they had a key, I didn't want them or the key to get away. I had the officers stay outside the block while I informed Officer Jones of the situation.

When I entered the block, I noticed that an inmate was using the universal weight machine in the bullpen. Each time he'd lift the weight he'd let it crash down, covering any sounds that the escapees were making. They'd also picked a time when the officers were tied up with other jobs, and would be less likely to see them.

I left the East Wing by the main door and joined the waiting officers who were by the ground level entrance. We had to go through three doors that were padlocked before reaching the hose room. Since we had to be fast, I had the officers go in order. The first officer would unlock the first door and stand aside to let the rest of us rush through. The same thing would be done for each of the other doors. Hopefully, we'd reach them before the expected warning shouts did.

Everything went as we'd planned, but when we reached the hose room, it was padlocked from the outside. Then I realized that the padlock could be reached through the bars of the bullpen. All the inmates had to do was give the key and the lock to a confederate in the bullpen who would, then, lock them inside.

When all the officers were assembled around the hose room door, I stood to the side and unlocked it.

Keeping our feet against it, we allowed it to open enough to see inside. My flashlight revealed three inmates who were trying their best to hide in the relatively empty room.

We had them back out, one at a time, handcuffed them, and placed all three in isolation. They wouldn't identify their confederate in the bullpen. The key was never found so all the locks that it fit had to be changed. In those days, we were issued a set of keys that we could take home with us. Each set contained that type of key. I later learned that several of these "take-home" sets were reported missing over the years. Most were found at home or in vehicles so that no one thought that it was important enough to go through the major expense of changing locks.

"Come With Me!"

The staff at Seyms Street was often faced with doing so many things at once that occasionally they overlooked or misinterpreted important information. An example of this happened to Officer Paul Rajotte one evening.

Paul drew the Boundover Block on this particular shift. This block was located outside of the East Wing, and was considered a better housing unit than that noisy block. Most of the inmates in the Boundover Block had had their cases held over to another court or court session or were in the process of a jury trial. They, therefore, tended to be incarcerated for a longer period than the inmates in the East Wing and, in most cases, got along better with staff.

One of the duties that the Boundover block officer had to

perform was to let inmates in and out of their cells for meals and recreation. Occasionally, an inmate might sleep through a meal call or recreation call. This usually meant that he was stuck in his cell for a while because most officers wouldn't climb back up all those flights of stairs unless the officer was a nice guy.

Paul was a nice guy. He didn't mind doing more than was required of him. Sometimes an inmate on a lower tier would ask him to take something to an inmate on another tier. Paul would do it, as long as it didn't interfere with other parts of his job, whereas, some other officers would refuse.

During the three hour evening recreation, inmates were allowed to return to their cells at regularly scheduled times (about once an hour). About fifteen minutes after Paul had climbed up and down the three flights of stairs to let inmates in and out of their cells, his supervisor had given him the numbers of two cells that he wanted searched. He was late for a chow relief that he was scheduled to make. As he walked passed the Boundover Block an inmate who was passing by said to him, "Some guys are trying to get out upstairs." Paul thought he said it in kind of a funny way. He almost whispered the information. As soon as that thought entered his mind, however, it was pushed aside as he wondered if he should climb those stairs or go about his other tasks. "Oh, what the hell!" he said, under his breath as he climbed to the second tier.

He walked around the second tier, checking the inmates who were locked in. No one asked to be let out. He climbed to the third tier. As he rounded a corner, he saw three inmates. One of them was standing on the shoulders of the other two. He had a tool in his hand, and was using it to pry the boards from the ceiling.

"SOME INMATES ARE TRYING TO GET OUT UP-STAIRS!" rang through his mind. Not, out of their cells, but, out of the jail! His mouth dropped open and the hair began to go up on the back of his neck. He was alone, without a radio. It was three stories down to the very hard concrete and they had a weapon. The inmates saw him while these things raced through his mind. The inmate jumped down—still holding the tool.

Acting like this was an everyday occurrence, Paul said the only thing that came to his mind: "Give me that thing and come with me." And, they did!

The Zapper

My academy class sat around the long tables in the mess hall of the Haddam Jail Training Center. We were one of the first forty classes to participate in this new concept of actually training correctional staff before putting them in an inmate environment.

From the minute we entered this old jail, we were told that failure to obey any rules or have an improper attitude would be grounds for immediate dismissal. We were appropriately cowed. Then the staff took all of our clothing, strip searched us, and locked us up for forty-eight hours.

Correctional thinking at that time was that the individual staff member had to undergo incarceration and the lowest form of treatment from their keepers to understand what inmates thought and felt. It was a decent simulation. We knew, however, that we'd done nothing wrong, it would end soon, and we could end it at anytime that it became unbearable to us.

Although the "lock-up phase" may have had some merit, the rest of our "training" left a lot to be desired. We were confronted with angry black men who told us that we were white honkys that would never understand a black's problems and druggies that extolled the virtues of the drug program that they were in while telling us that we'd never understand their problem. Several of us wondered why—other than the money that these "angry blacks," and the "good-time" that these "poor druggies" received—would they bother to take the time to lecture us poor incorrigibles?

After the third group of druggies had addressed us, I opened my mouth (forever endearing myself to a counselor who would eventually become a deputy commissioner).

I asked the inmate panel, " We have heard from a number of inmates in programs like yours who have said the same, programmed things. If you really believe what you are saying, how long after you're released do you think this brainwashing is going to last?" The inmates didn't answer, but this counselor jumped up and berated my "attitude." I, later, received a "periodic review" that said that I'd never last in corrections as I had a "poor attitude."

As we sat around the long table, Training Captain Gimianni explained that we were going to cover the topic of "frisks" or "pat searches." At this point, we didn't know our classmates. It was shortly after the lock-up phase and we hadn't had time to socialize. Those of us who had worked at institutions before being assigned to this class did realize that half the class were not correctional officers. The dress code, at that time, would not have allowed the long hair and scruffy appearance of half of our classmates.

As the instruction proceeded, Training Captain Gimianni said, "I have asked one of your classmates to hide various items of contraband on his person. I will ask some of you to come up and find those items during a routine pat-frisk.

The man seated next to me stood up to act the part of an inmate. Another classmate did a pat-frisk and found about five items. The student who had performed the frisk was very thorough, and few wanted to risk failure when we were informed that the first trainee hadn't found all of the contraband. Finally, two or three of my classmates got up and found about three more items. The training captain then told the student who was portraying the inmate to remove the rest of the items and place them on the table. He proceeded to put about twenty items in front of us.

The training captain then asked our classmate to explain his background. He listed the times that he had been incarcerated. Many of us were dumbfounded. Inmates in our class? What goes on here?

Training Captain Gimianni explained that the department felt that the best people to counsel drug offenders (which were 86% of our population) were ex-druggies. He went on to say that a third of our class were people from this group who would go to different institutions to perform this counseling function.

During the next few weeks I spent some time with the ex-offender who had played the part of the inmate for the pat-frisk class. I found that he was a warm, knowledgeable person. He helped me understand much more than the lock-up phase did. I called him "Zapper."

I was standing by the A&P, four years later, when Zapper came by. He was wearing an unsentenced inmate's brown uniform. He'd lost thirty pounds since I'd last seen him. His face was pale with a scraggly stubble.

When I finally recognized him, I said, "Zapper, what are you doing here?" He looked at me, knowing he'd seen me before, but not knowing where. In a slow, tired voice he said, "Sarge, it's not good that we talk here. The other inmates wouldn't understand. Call me down to your office later."

Later that night, I talked with him for two hours. He'd been laid off from his counseling job (budget cut backs) and went back to drugs. I never tried to use him as an informant. Somehow that would have betrayed something. He went to court and was sentenced to spend some time with us.

An "All Available Officers" call brought me to the Old Jail one night. This was where the sentenced inmates lived. Zapper was among them. The medical team and several officers had arrived before I did. As I glanced into the cell where they were working, I saw Zapper lying on the floor with a hypodermic still stuck in his vein.

We carried him out the front door. He had regained consciousness and seemed okay. An hour later he was dead in the hospital. Darvon overdose. He had gathered Darvon pills from other inmates, street sources, or wherever. Patiently, he had ground them down, dissolved them in water, and injected them into his body with a much used hypo. What a waste! What could he have been?

The Pitter-Patter of Little Feet

In jails everywhere, the on-coming shifts' supervisors usually arrive early enough to get a briefing on the previous twenty four hour's activities from the on-duty shift. Lieutenant Jim Barton and I arrived early one evening for this reason. As we entered the jail, we noticed that there was a big clean-up effort going on in the Medical Wing. This was unusual enough to be the subject of our first question to the day shift supervisor.

We were told that an inmate name Rafael Sanchez had gone nuts and torn out the plumbing in his Medical Wing cell when officers went to get him to take him to court that morning. He had done such a good job that the whole wing was flooded and it took hours to repair. The supervisor's last

37

words on the matter were, "You guys won't have to worry about him. I'm sure they'll take him to Norwich (the State Mental Hospital) after his court appearance."

The evening was going pretty smoothly when, a few hours later, Officer Tom Knapp called from A&P Room. "I think you guys better get over here," he said in a nonplused way. When we'd strolled over to the A&P Room we noticed that he had cleared it of all inmates. Even the inmate janitors were gone although they had obviously not finished cleaning. "What's up, Tom?"

He looked at us in a baleful way and said, "More than you know."

He went on to tell us that he was finishing booking the last few inmates when he realized that he couldn't find the last man that he'd sent into the shower. He went into the shower and noticed a ceiling tile was moved in the low, suspended ceiling. He figured that the inmate had moved the tile, stood on the new handicapped hand rails, and raised himself onto the suspended ceiling. I asked if he'd heard the inmate trying to break out. He said that the inmate had been pretty quiet, but that just before we got there he could hear him moving around.

Lieutenant Barton asked how the ceiling was supporting him. Tom said that he didn't know other than that the inmate was pretty small and seemed to be walking on the cross members. Lieutenant Barton asked the inmate's name. Rafael Sanchez was the reply. We looked at each other and said, "Oh shit!"

While the lieutenant tried to talk to Rafael we called for a Spanish-speaking officer and a ladder. Officer Ed Faber brought the ladder and volunteered to try to locate the inmate by sticking his head up above the false ceiling. I told him to get a helmet and some Mace first. In the meantime, Rafael refused to answer either the lieutenant or the Spanish-speaking officer.

When Officer Faber returned, we were standing around, scratching our heads, and looking stupid. "Another fine mess you've gotten me in, Ollie." Ed climbed the ladder and removed a panel in an area that we thought was distant from the inmate's present position. As he cautiously popped his head up he said, "I can see the son-of-a-bitch in the corner. He's got some kind of a metal bar in his hand." Lieutenant Barton and I looked at each other and shrugged. He said, "Mace him!" After the Mace was used, we waited and tried again to talk to the inmate. Officer Faber reported that the Mace didn't seem to have any effect.

While all of this was going on, Officer Knapp was thinking the situation over and leaning on a push broom. He looked down at the push broom and said, "Lieutenant, I can get him down." Lieutenant Barton asked how he was going to do that and Tom said, "Just give me room."

He walked over to an area near where the inmate was last seen and said, "Hey shithead, come down now or I'm going to shove this broomstick up your ass." When there was no reaction, he jammed the stick through an overhead tile. The inmate reacted to that by moving a few feet and giving away his new position. Tom started moving after him, jabbing holes through the tiles. Round and round they went! After ten minutes the inmate took a wrong step—he probably found it hard to step carefully while protecting certain areas—and fell through some tiles. The first words out of his mouth upon landing in an ignoble pile were, "*¡No mas! ¡No mas!*"

Only after Rafael was handcuffed and taken away did we notice the devastation. Almost every ceiling tile in a ceiling of fifty by sixty feet was destroyed. With the dust in the air it looked like a bomb had exploded. The only bright thing in the room was Tom Knapp's smile as he stood, holding his broom.

Lieutenant Barton said, "How do I explain this to the boss?" This caused a lot of eyes to be averted, some clearing of throats, and a sudden need to be elsewhere for most of us. I said, "No problem." I picked up an imaginary phone and said, "Boss, how are you doing? Trouble? No, we didn't have any trouble. I just called to see how you were doing. Oh, by the way, we wrecked your fucking A&P Room." Then I quickly hung up. Everyone but the lieutenant thought that was funny. The real conversation (at least the side I heard) went a little differently.

"Boss, ah, we ah had a problem."

"No, no, everything is...ah, quiet now."

"Well you know that ceiling that used to be above the A&P?"

I never heard the rest of that conversation because the lieutenant slammed his office door to keep out the sound of laughter.

The Hole

"The Hole" was the common name for the jail-within-a-jail. It was a place to put inmates who couldn't function within the jail society, and showed this by assaulting, fighting, or trying to escape.

The proper name for this housing assignment was "Maximum Punitive Segregation." All the staff knew the correct name, but we still called it the Hole.

Around 1968, all jails and prisons within the state were united under the Department of Correction. This meant that they were no longer fully autonomous. They, now, had to abide by a set of rules called Administrative Directives. One of the things that those directives controlled was the assignment to Maximum Punitive Segregation.

In the days when Seyms Street was a county jail, any officer could put someone in the Hole, and that inmate would stay there until that officer said he could come out. No inmate would mess with an officer who he knew was going on a three week vacation. The inmates knew what that would mean—three weeks of bread and water.

With the formation of the department, definite parameters were established with regard to the type of incident that the inmate had to be involved in, the staff who could authorize an inmate being so housed, and the length of time an inmate could be kept in the Hole. Old-time staff didn't like that one bit.

The Hole at Seyms Street would be considered cruel and unusual punishment these days. However, it sure did work to change violent behavior. It had four cells that sat above the jail's furnace. The furnace ran all year long to provide hot water. The temperature in the Hole during summer was often a hundred degrees.

To enter the Hole you unlocked a half-inch-thick steel door. As the door opened, the only lights went on. Ahead of you there was a corridor with four cells on the right side. The doors to these cells were tightly spaced bars that had a pass-through on the bottom.

The insides of the cells contained a cot that was bolted to the wall, a mattress that was removed during the daylight hours, and a five gallon plastic bucket for sanitary purposes. The cells themselves were narrow and not too deep. The only ventilation came from a twelve-inch fan that was mounted in the wall. That fan also let in the only light to be had when the main door was closed. When the door was closed you could, quite literally, not see your hand in front of your face. The inmates in the Hole had to be checked by an officer twice each hour, once each shift by a shift supervisor, and daily by the medical staff.

There was never any certainty as to how an inmate would react to being put in the Hole. Some would come out with a whole new outlook on their past behavior. Some would go right back to doing the things that got them put in there in the first place. A few couldn't take it (especially if the other cells were empty). They would plead with every staff member that visited to be released. They were all happy to leave.

One summer we had four inmates in the Hole. They borrowed bravery from each other's behavior and were doing everything possible to be disruptive. They'd take a portion of each of their meals and throw it through the bars where it stuck to bars, walls, and the corridor floor. The contents of their plastic cans soon followed. By the third day of their stay in our hotel it took a strong-stomached staff member to open the main door. The stench was overwhelming! That was the night that Officer Grant (not his real name) had to check the Hole every half hour.

Officer Grant had two attributes that determined much of his behavior. He was built like a football lineman and he had a very short fuse. All that evening, he complained to Lieutenant Barton and me about the smell in the Hole until he got permission to take a volunteer inmate in to clean it.

Lieutenant Barton and I were in the lieutenants' office when Grant started this monumental task. The inmate that was helping him had learned the true meaning of the axiom, "never volunteer." He was turning progressive shades of green. His motivation was further dimmed by the threats coming from the inmates in the Hole, one of which was to give anyone who entered a shitcan bath.

Officer Grant went in, trying not to slip on the foul mixture that coated the floor, and confronted each of them. I'm not sure what he told them, but they agreed not to interfere with his cleanup efforts.

I could watch his progress from my seat in the lieutenants' office, but I was paying little attention as I was talking with Lieutenant Barton at the same time. I noticed that they'd swept and were now gingerly picking up the debris. Later, I saw Grant wielding a mop. I happened to look up in time to see him empty a gallon of what looked like bleach when the inmates in the Hole began to shout. I jumped up, and followed by Lieutenant Barton, went to investigate.

When I reached the Hole the smell of ammonia hit me. I said to Grant, "What the hell did you do?" He told me that even after he'd swept and mopped the stink was still so bad that he decided to add some ammonia and bleach. I saw the two empty bottles on the ground.

At the same time, the lieutenant called some officers out of the officers' mess hall. With their help we were able to get the inmates out of the Hole and under a shower. Luckily, none were burned or otherwise injured.

Officer Grant couldn't understand why everyone was upset with what he'd done. We, naturally, watched him a lot closer from then on. He was terminated from state service a while later.

The Man with the Toothpick

No matter what kind of work you do, you will occasionally meet someone that you can point to and say, "That person is the one we should hold up to the new people as a shining example." That person will have our respect and admiration. In small and sometimes feeble ways we attempt to emulate their behavior, and hope to someday be the same kind of example for our peers. To me, in my Seyms Street days, Officer Billy Lynch was such a person.

Billy use to be a professional boxer. He left that before his brains were scrambled. Some said he left after refusing to throw a match. I can believe that.

I don't remember the time we first met, but I do recall those times when I'd have to explain something to Billy. I always had the feeling that I had to get him on my side when that happened. He'd look at me, moving the toothpick in his mouth, and he'd evaluate me. If I was right in what I'd said, Billy would move the toothpick to the other side of his mouth and nod—sometimes adding a smile, if he really agreed. If I was wrong, he'd say so, but in a straightforward, and, yes, diplomatic way.

Physically, Billy wasn't that tall or that muscular. He was a black man who stood about five foot ten or eleven, weighed about 180 pounds. He was the kind of person who didn't age. He could have been in his late thirties or early forties. He didn't strut when he walked—as well he could have. He'd walk normally, sometimes with his head down, hand to his mouth, as he worried that toothpick. Billy never talked about his private life. He was a bachelor.

One night I received a call from a lieutenant on the Hartford Police Department. He told me that they were looking for a corrections officer who had come to the aid of two Hartford police officers at a McDonald's. They wanted to thank the officer, but also wanted a statement from him because the people who were arrested were complaining that the H.P.D. officers had used excessive force. I asked the time and location of the incident. Checking past rosters, I determined that Billy was the only one who would have gone home that way on that night. When I asked him about it he refused to meet my eyes, smiled, and said, "It wasn't me." I had to tell the H.P.D. lieutenant that none of my people were involved and that he should check other institutions because we all wore the same uniform.

If Billy had one shortcoming, I think it was in his report writing (probably because he didn't have to write many reports). He would handle most situations with the force of his personality and knowledge. There was one time when talking didn't work.

An arrestee had been admitted after the A&P closed. Apparently, neither the arresting officer nor the accepting officer had done a good job of searching him because he had a knife. He was seated on a bench near the Control Center, waiting to be processed. An officer stopped at the Control Center to speak to Officer Al Monico Sr. When he turned to leave, the arrestee was standing there with a knife pointed at his throat.

Billy had gone to the A&P to use the pay phone. When he returned, he rounded a corner and found the other officer standing there with a knife to his throat. Billy approached slowly. The arrestee became more agitated when he found he was facing two officers. The knife went from one to the other. Billy and the other officer were trying to talk him out of the knife. Suddenly, Billy struck! Witnesses told me that they had never seen hands move so fast. No one could accurately say how many times the inmate was hit, but he dropped the knife and was unconscious. I'm sure Billy must have moved the toothpick to the other side of his mouth and smiled.

Don't Mess!

One of the things that should never in any way be tainted in any institution is the food. Both staff and inmates get very upset at even a rumor that someone has done something unsanitary with their food.

One evening, a rumor spread through Seyms Street that a mouse had run through the food on the serving line, and had been killed by someone hitting it with a serving spoon. According to the rumor, this was the food that we were about to serve for supper.

The staff didn't know anything about this rumor as we manned our posts in the mess hall. Then we began to get reports from various blocks that said that the inmates were going to refuse to eat. Lieutenant Barton investigated the matter. He found that there may have been some truth to the rumor, but that no staff had witnessed the alleged event. To the annoyance of the cook, he ordered the food on the line to be replaced. Then he told the block officers to inform the inmates in their area of what he had done. Inmates began to trickle into the mess hall, but tensions were high.

A fight broke out in the middle of the dining hall. Inmates gathered around the combatants, hindering the staff's attempts to intervene. Sergeant George Howard, Officer Ed Adams, and other officers were able to break through the crowd and start to restore order. Sergeant Howard had one of the fighters by the foot. He raised the foot up, suspending the inmate in a vertical position. "Let go of my foot!" the inmate wailed. "I ain't decided that it's still yours," replied the sergeant.

C/O Ed Adams wrapped his arms around the other fighter and started to drag him backward. A fist flew from the crowd and hit Ed in the head. He went down. No one saw who threw the punch.

The crowd in the dining room rose to their feet and began shouting, "Kill the bastards!" Lieutenant Barton and I were by the entrance door, facing the crowd. A salt shaker sailed over the crowd and hit the lieutenant in the forehead. Dazed and bleeding, he backed out into the hallway as more staff arrived to control the situation. He shook off the pain and returned to the dining hall to resume command. We nearly lost the institution because of a rumor.

Inmates aren't the only ones who react when someone messes with their food. Prior to my working at Seyms Street, there was a sergeant who angered other staff in a number of ways. Some of his reported antics included adding large quantities of pepper to an officer's food when the officer left the table to wash his hands, and taking an officer's meal when the officer got up to get some milk. Payback is a bitch!

One evening, two officers decided that it was time for revenge. When the sergeant was about to sit down to his cheeseburger meal, one officer went into the lieutenants' office and called his fellow conspirator who was assigned to a block. He then came out of the office and called the sergeant to the telephone. While the officer in the block held the sergeant's attention, the first officer put a small dead mouse in the sergeant's cheeseburger.

The sergeant was somewhat surprised to find that all the officers who had been eating when he went to the phone had finished eating, and left the mess hall.

He didn't know that someone was spying on him. He sat down to resume his interrupted meal. He picked up the cheeseburger in both hands. Just as he was opening his mouth, bringing the cheeseburger closer, the mouse's tail fell out and swung back and forth.

The eyewitness swears that the sergeant turned chalk white and dropped the cheeseburger back to his plate. His color tended toward the greenish end of the color spectrum after he removed the top of the bun. He made an express stop in the bathroom, not even closing the door to cover the sound of his retching.

Years later, when I heard the story, I asked one of the plotters if he would have really allowed the sergeant to take that bite. He said, "Of course not!" His smile gave me a different answer.

"Once Upon A Time..."

Although most modern prison administrators will tell you that their institutions do not have a snitch system, few will deny that their jails and prisons rely on inmates giving staff information. What the administrators mean is that they don't have an established system that rewards informants. They fear that an overt, systematic approach to intelligence gathering will result in harm to the informants (which happened in the New Mexico State Prison riot), and may lower the quality of the reported information because other inmates will not talk to known snitches.

However, as I said before, no institution can expect to operate smoothly without regular information from inmate sources. Informants may be muscle-bound, tattoo-wearing bikers or someone who looks like they're doing a Wally Cox imitation. You never know.

Most correctional staff are continuously gathering information. They are alert to attitude changes in the inmates with which they regularly deal, and are receptive to approaches from any inmate that may lead to important information.

On one evening watch at Seyms Street, an officer called me to ask if I, or the lieutenant, would speak to an inmate. He said that he thought this inmate had "only one oar in the water," but he couldn't be certain. The inmate was very convincing.

Inmate Sam Barnet arrived at the lieutenant's office a few minutes later. He was a small, thin black man whose eyes were always on the move, yet he did not appear to be nervous. The next few minutes of conversation had me questioning my own sanity. Sam matter-of-factly explained that he was with the C.I.A. and was working on a case. He was totally convincing and even volunteered to provide us with a phone number so that we could call his boss. He reeled off a series of digits that he claimed were his agent number.

When the lieutenant asked what he wanted with us he explained that there was a lot of drug activity going on in the jail. He felt he could help us curb it with some information. We wanted to know why he would do this. He insinuated that the chaos caused by the drug activity was interfering with "something I'm working on."

Although we were highly skeptical about Sam's story, we took down the telephone number and his "agent number" (which he repeated twice without making a mistake). He, also, gave us the name of a local detective who he "had worked with before" and who would vouch for him.

Then we asked what information he had for us. He asked if we knew Inmate Douglas Johnson. When I said that I knew him, he said that Inmate Johnson was carrying some drugs in a cigarette package inside his pocket. He went on to say that they were pills that he got from "the outside." As he left, he mentioned that Johnson was up in Shop 3 (the recreation area for sentenced inmates).

Shop 3 was going to close for the night in a few minutes. I told the lieutenant that I'd wait by the hallway door and have Johnson step into the office when he came by. A few minutes later, I ushered a bewildered Johnson into the lieutenants' office.

Johnson said, "What's this all about? What you want with me?" I reminded him that it was institutional policy that the custodial staff had to do shakedowns (searches) of two inmates each shift, and that he was going to help me fill my quota. I told him to empty his pockets and turn around.

He whined about being "picked on," but complied with my order. No cigarette pack! I proceeded to frisk him and felt something in his pocket. I said, "I told you to empty your pockets. What have you got in there?" A look of panic crossed his face and he bolted for the door.

The door to the hallway was made up of fine mesh screening and was primarily intended to keep inmates out of the staff dining hall which was adjacent to the lieutenants' office. It had a small house-type lock that was easily opened from the inside for the staff's convenience. I reached Johnson just as he reached the door and opened it. He was screaming, "Help!" to his buddies who were passing in the corridor.

I slammed the door closed and tried to control Johnson. Lieutenant Barton had his other arm, but was having trouble keeping his balance due to an ankle that he had previously sprained. We could hear the inmates screaming in the hallway, "Let him go!" We didn't want to use any more force on him than to hold his arms, because we knew that would cause a riot. So there we were—being swung around the little anteroom by a large inmate who continued to whine for help. Every time he'd free one of his arms he'd make a lunge for the door's lock. Eventually he made it. I tried to press against the door to keep the inmates out, but there were too many of them. About twenty inmates came in and pulled him away from us. We stood there panting and overwhelmed with surprise that they had been so audacious and that we were uninjured in the process.

About fifteen minutes after the inmates ran off, Sam

appeared at the office. He offered to get the drugs for us. He returned a few minutes later with a mangled cigarette box filled with pills. Fearing that he had compromised himself, we asked how he'd gotten them. He explained that he'd followed Johnson as he ran away, and saw Johnson throw the box in the trash. He told us not to worry about him because Johnson "thinks I'm his friend."

We later checked with the detective that Sam had given as a reference. He described Sam as "a flake," but admitted that Sam had given him some good information in the past. We were too embarrassed to call the C.I.A. number.

ZZZZZZZZZ

The heart of most security procedures in jails is the count. Most institutions have a minimum of five official counts, and several more that are scheduled on a random basis.

During counts, inmates are expected to stand quietly by their beds unless they are already asleep in them. They are not to move around or do anything to distract the officer. If they are sleeping, the officer is instructed to make sure that he/she sees "living, breathing flesh." Many unusual occurrences centered around counts.

Old-timers told me about the time when an inmate was counted (several times) as he sat on the toilet. The only trouble was that he was dead. He'd died while communing with Nature and the many officers who counted him thought nothing of the fact that he was always on the pot when they passed his cell.

The most unusual incident that happened at Seyms Street while I was there was the bad count of the Work Release Inmates.

At one time Seyms Street was the county jail for Hartford County. The jail was run by an elected sheriff and his appointed deputies. The sheriff had living quarters above the Control Center. When the jails were absorbed into the Department of Correction, these living quarters were given over to a work release program.

The inmates assigned to work release were supervised by a counselor during the day. They were expected to return from work at a set time and weren't allowed to leave after they returned from work. In the evenings and nights the only supervision they received was an occasional visit from a staff member.

On this particular evening, Officer Al Monico Sr. was in the Control Center. Part of his job was to receive the count figures from the officers in various areas, compare them to a master count figure, and tell the officer if he had a correct count or had to recount his area. Sometimes mistakes occurred when the Control Center officer was not informed of a bed change or a discharge, but most of the time the master figure was correct. Most errors were the fault of the officer taking a count.

Officer Eddie Colon was assigned to count the work release area. Just before count time he'd been sneaking a peek at a football game on TV. His favorite team, the Buffalo Bills, were playing. Eddie pronounced it "Boo-fa-loo Bills" to the merriment of anyone within hearing range.

Eddie walked up the long flight of stairs to the work release area. As he reached the top, he shouted, "Count," and waited while the inmates scurried to their individual beds. Then he went from room to room, counting the inmates in each. When he was finished, he returned to the Control Center to give his count to Officer Monaco. He wanted to get it over fast so he could return to the game.

"Work release has twenty-five inmates."

"That's wrong. There should only be twenty-four. I'll double check my figures while you recount."

Eddie trudged back up the long flight of stairs, caught his breath at the top, and announced, "Recount." While he waited for the inmates to return to their rooms, he was slightly embarrassed by shouts like: "Can't even fucking count"; "Take your shoes off so you can use your toes"; "Give us a break! We're watching the game." The inmates reluctantly moved to their assigned area. This time, as he went from room to room, he was a little more careful. "Yes, that was someone in bed; not a pile of clothes," he thought. He, also, made sure that he noted what beds were empty in each room. "Sheet! I still got twenty-five." He returned to the Control Center, hoping that Officer Monico had made a mistake and corrected it. He'd really rub it in if that happened. He'd make Al pay for making him miss part of the game.

"I still got twenty-five in work release."

"I checked my figures. You should have twenty-four. Take the picture file with you, and check each face."

Eddie took the file and started back to the stairs. He stopped at the bottom and thought, "Fucking stairs are looking longer." He walked up the stairs, all the bounce out of his step and leaning heavily on the railing. He didn't bother to announce that he was counting this time; but went from each area to the other, checking faces against pictures.

As he approached the last room, he realized that he was out of pictures; but he swore that there had been someone sleeping in one of the beds. He turned on the light, pulled back the covers, and discovered Sergeant Jefferson snoring away.

"Sarge, Sarge. Wake up! Madre! What do I do now?"

The sergeant and he returned to the Control Center and explained that Eddie had counted the sergeant by mistake. He didn't mention that the sergeant was asleep on duty. For weeks after that he was the brunt of every jokester on the shift. They were constantly giving him vision checks and mentioning that they'd never heard of a color blind person who couldn't see blue (the color of our uniform shirts). He suffered the bantering in his good natured way, but didn't tell.

Sarge

"Sarge" was the nickname of one of our inmates. He was what is now called a "street person." In the last days of Seyms Street, this type of person was often referred to as a "balky." That name means a person who lives on the streets because of an alcohol problem.

There were many rumors about Sarge's history. Some said that he had been a sergeant in the army, had been a hero in one war or another, and received a pension from the government. None of this was provable because Sarge didn't communicate much, and when he did, he didn't talk about himself.

I first saw Sarge as I walked down the hallway in the jail. He was picking cigarette butts off of the floor. My attention was drawn to him because after he picked up a flattened butt he stuck it into the corner of his mouth and searched his pocket for a light. As I approached to ask what he was doing (I was a new sergeant at the time and didn't know that this was normal street behavior), he said, "Give me a light, motherfucker." I was taken back because this was not the language that an inmate normally used toward staff.

I sensed that there was something different about this inmate, so I held my tongue and gave him a light.

His first drag on the butt left him little more than the filter. He looked at me. The expression in his eyes was flat, like he'd seen too much in his life. After a long moment he grunted, "Humph," and turned away. As he searched for another butt he kept up a mumbled conversation with himself.

I was curious about him, and asked one of the staff who he was and what was his history. That's when I first heard all the rumors about Sarge. I was never able to prove or disprove any of them.

Physically, Sarge was a tall, thin, black man. Even he didn't know how old he was. He walked with a head down, shuffling step. Sarge made a habit of looking people up and down as if he were sizing them up. He would usually not look into your eyes unless he was angry. At those times, his stare was like looking down the barrels of a shotgun.

During my five years in two different jails, I saw Sarge booked-in hundreds of times. He was doing a life sentence on the installment plan. Usually, when the Hartford police brought him in, the booking officer would utter a moan of despair. He knew that Sarge would have to be strip searched, and wasn't looking forward to handling Sarge's clothing.

I watched the officers going through this process with Sarge once. Sarge knew the procedure and considered it an affront if the officer was inept enough to try to tell him what to take off next or where to pile his clothing. At such times he would stop stripping and glare at the officer. No amount of persuasion could get him started again until he was ready.

On the occasion that I was watching, I'm sure that I must

have had a bewildered expression on my face. As I watched, Sarge took off his pants only to reveal another pair underneath. He was also wearing three pairs of socks and four shirts. It dawned on me that all that clothing was needed to protect him from the cold of that winter night. Sarge didn't smell too good. He'd been out of jail for two weeks, and there are no showers on the street. None of the officers liked to search Sarge or his clothing, but we knew that it was necessary. Sarge had once been booked-in with two steak knives stuck in his socks. Even then, the police didn't want to touch him to search him.

Sarge was a loner. The other inmates were afraid of his potential for violence. One told me to watch Sarge's pants. If they were worn normally, everything was all right. If, on the other hand, he tucked them into his socks, puttee-style, he was "losing his cool" and might become violent.

During recreation, Sarge would stand to the side and watch. It looked like he was supervising the other inmates. Sometimes he would sprawl in a chair, legs crossed, muttering to himself.

In the mess hall, Sarge would go through the chow line and then pick an unoccupied table. After he put his tray down, he would sit back, looking at his food as if trying to decide if he wanted to eat it. After a while he'd move his chair up and reach for the pepper shaker. He'd pour out about a quarter of the pepper onto his food, put the shaker down, stare at his food, and pick up the shaker to put on still more pepper. Only the unknowing would sit at Sarge's table.

Anyone with the temerity to interrupt his eating ritual would find that Sarge would jump up, knocking his chair over, and start shouting at him. After the intruder moved, Sarge would continue mumbling and pick up his chair. He'd slam the chair down, ignore his food, and glower at the offender (who was usually several tables away by then).

Sarge rarely was any real problem for the staff. Most of the time he just wanted his meals, bed, and to be left alone. He never had any money, but the only thing he would have bought from the commissary were cigarettes. We would provide him with Bugler or Tops tobacco and rolling papers, free, so he didn't need to go to the commissary. At one point we noticed that some inmates were using the free rolling papers to make joints with smuggled marijuana. The administration decided to stop issuing Tops and Bugler to make it more difficult to engage in that illegal activity. That caused Sarge to throw a fit. It was finally decided that we'd supply him with the makings, but only after he swore not to let anyone else have the papers. Serenity returned to the jail with that decision.

Sarge was as much a part of Seyms Street as the doors and windows. I saw him often at the new jail we moved to that replaced Seyms Street. He seemed to be out of his natural environment.

After I moved on to another institution, I would ask about him whenever I met an officer from the jail. The officer would always smile and say, "Old Sarge, yeah, he still comes to visit us." One day I asked that question of an officer who was at old Seyms Street with me. He said, "Didn't you hear? Sarge died!" He probably thought I acted funny because I didn't want to hear about the circumstances. I just wanted to be alone to think about old Sarge and Seyms Street.

"All Available Officers..."

Someone described law enforcement as "Hours and hours of boredom interspersed by moments of sheer terror." At Seyms Street, adrenaline began its flow with the words, "All available officers..." This was announced over the P.A. system and was followed by a location. The call was only used for emergencies and was a guarantee that the officer needing help would get plenty of manpower, rapidly.

Some types of emergencies happened more often in certain locations. If you heard an "all available" call to a housing unit, it usually involved a fight. A call to the hospital was often due to an inmate trying to hang himself. Because each staff that responds to these calls is rushing into the unknown, we always warned new staff to arrive rapidly, but with caution.

Friday nights at Seyms Street marked a transition period. All week long, staff was involved with discharging inmates and booking-in replacements. After the booking was finished on Friday night, the jail changed gears for the weekend schedule. Few inmates were brought in or let go on the weekend. People who were arrested on Saturday or Sunday were usually held in the police department's lock-up.

This Friday night was no different than others before it. The only exception to that was that we had many more staff on duty than was normal. Seyms Street was about to close forever. The new jail at Weston Street would need more staff. We were training these new officers on the four to twelve watch. All of them were transfers from places like the maximum security prison at Somers.

All of the inmates that had been brought in that day had been processed. One inmate was sitting on the bench by the Control Center. He was waiting for his bondsman to fill out some papers so he could go home.

Shortly before lock-up, at 9 P.M., the call came over the P.A. system, "All available officers to the hospital!"

As I arrived at the hospital's entrance, the Control Center officer opened the door electrically. I burst through the door and came face-to-face with one of the inmate janitors who worked in our infirmary. He was holding up his hand to signal us to stop. At first I thought that he had accidentally hit the panic alarm's switch. He came running to me, however, and said, "Don't go in there. They're holding the medic hostage."

I told Officer Fred Gibson, who'd transferred in from Somers that week, to stop everyone at the door. Then I questioned the janitor. After he'd told me that the inmates and Medic Louis Cucia were in the bullpen (the recreation area), I cautiously looked around the corner. There stood the medic, tied up in strips of sheets. An inmate was standing behind him, holding a shiv (homemade knife) to his throat. Both of them were behind the eight-foot-high fence that was used to keep inmates in the bullpen.

As Lieutenant Dave Brown arrived to take charge, two

other inmates with shivs moved to stand behind their leader. All were young, white, and looked scared. After I had quickly briefed him, Lieutenant Brown said, "I'm going to try to talk with them and see if that gate is locked. See if you can find the spare key in the warden's office." As I exited the hospital, I told the gathered officers what was happening and warned them to not allow themselves to be seen for fear that they would scare the hostage-takers into action. I sent some of them to assist in locking up the other housing units, and went to look for the spare key.

The key coding system left a question in my mind as to whether or not I had found the correct spare. When I returned with the one I thought was right, I voiced those concerns to Lieutenant Brown. He had already determined that the gate was locked. He also told me that the inmates had just arrived from Whiting Forensic (the state's mental facility for violent criminals). He went to start the emergency call-in of the warden and other necessary staff.

The inmates had demanded to be returned to Whiting, to talk with the warden, and to talk with the commissioner. When he returned, Lieutenant Brown attempted to keep the inmates talking. I had gotten permission from him to arm the officers with nightsticks and Mace. The waiting began.

In those days, no one in the department was trained as a hostage negotiator. Our training did not include the tactics for hostage rescue, either. The only equipment we had were the nightsticks and a few different types of chemical agent. We knew, however, that it might come down to a rescue operation if the hostage's safety was endangered.

In a short while, the people that Lieutenant Brown had called in began to arrive. Among them was Deputy Commissioner Lopes, Jail Administrator Coyle, Warden Wezowicz, and Dr. Serafini.

Warden Wezowicz and Deputy Commissioner Lopes did not come into the hospital area. One of the hostage-takers demands was to see them. Lieutenant Brown was able to stall by saying that he had called for them, but that they hadn't arrived yet. They monitored the activity with the TV camera that covered that area in the Control Center. They sent in Jail Administrator Coyle because his name and position were not well known to the inmates.

Mr. Coyle and Lieutenant Brown discussed tactics. They set up an order of attack with the staff, and a key phrase that either would say to trigger the officers' assault. Lieutenant Brown reported that they no longer had the medic by the gate. He was now sitting on a picnic table to the back of the bullpen. They noticed that as Lieutenant Brown said something that interested them, the two inmates that were guarding the medic seemed to forget that he was there. They'd move toward the gate to listen better or throw in their own comments. They even got to the point where they untied the medic's hands. Mr. Coyle suggested that they try the "good cop, bad cop" routine on them to make them forget about the hostage and move closer to the gate.

Earlier, while we were talking about the assault phase, it was decided that if or when it came, the first few officers would round the corner, jump onto some filing cabinets that were next to the fence, and jump over. In the meantime, Lieutenant Brown would try the key in the gate. If it opened, everyone else would rush through. If it didn't, everyone would use the cabinet route.

As Lieutenant Brown, who played "good cop," started talking, I spoke with Mr. Coyle. I convinced him that we needed someone outside of the window with a firearm to cover the medic when the assault started. After thinking about it for a while, he gave his permission. I sent an officer for a ladder, and told him to notify me when he got it to the Control Center. In the meantime, I watched as Mr. Coyle barged in on Lieutenant Brown and said some things to stir up the hostage-takers. When he returned to where we were he said that it had worked. The hostage-takers all came to the gate to curse at him.

I got the call that the ladder was ready, and went to the Control Center to draw my pistol from the armory. As I was doing this, Deputy Commissioner Lopes stopped me. He said that if shooting becomes a possibility, we'd call in the state police. I rolled my eyes upward, looking toward heaven, in the hopes that I would be provided with a good argument to be used on him. As I did so, my eyes stopped on the TV monitor in time to see Officer Perry Davis vaulting the fence.

I yelled, "They're attacking!" and ran to the gate to enter the institution. In the hospital, I rounded the corner in time to see Officer Davis rolling on the ground with one of the inmates. The inmate still held his knife, and had it dangerously close to Officer Davis's throat. I kicked the inmate in the head, knocking him unconscious. I turned in time to see the warden coming through the gate and thought, "Well, so much for being a sergeant." I never knew whether or not he'd seen me, but nothing was ever said about my actions.

After the inmate was handcuffed, I turned to see how everyone else was. I heard the officers yelling, "Where did the fuckers go?" Then someone yelled, "They're on the third tier!" About twenty officers thundered up the steps to search all the unlocked cells. It became apparent, in a short while, that they weren't successful. Lieutenant Brown tried the handle on a wooden storage cabinet. It wouldn't open, so he began to kick it in. Others joined him and the cabinet was soon a pile of splinters. Lieutenant Brown stood in the middle of the pile with a confused look on his face. He'd been positive that the other two inmates were in there. They were finally found, hiding under the bunks of two cells on the first tier.

No staff members were hurt during the incident.

Dr. Serafini and Medic Cucia stitched up the inmate who'd tried to kill Officer Davis. Officer Gibson (the new transferee) turned to me, shaking his head, and said, "Holy shit! This place is like Dodge City. What did I get myself into?"

"Oh, God! Help!"

Corrections officers sometimes had to transport inmates to court or doctor appointments. We tried not to let the inmates know when they were going on medical trips because we found that their family or friends would often meet them at the hospital or doctor's office for an unauthorized visit. This wasn't possible with all court trips. The inmate was informed of the date by the court.

One day, Officer Phil Dorsch drew escort duty. He had an even larger than normal smile on his cheerful face. Escort duty was usually considered a "plum" job. It allowed the officer to get out of the jail for the day and to see the court proceedings.

Phil was taking four inmates to court. He drew leg irons

and belly chains, and went to the A&P Room. The inmates had been dressed in their civilian clothing for court, and were patiently waiting. Phil checked the paperwork to make sure that it was complete. Then he chained the inmates, drew lunches for them, and escorted them to his waiting car.

For security purposes, inmates were loaded and unloaded into vehicles in an enclosed courtyard. The rule was that the sliding gate was kept closed during those times. This would prevent an inmate from getting a head start if he decided to run. After his inmates were in the car and the doors were locked, Phil signaled for the gate to be opened.

As he slowly backed onto the street, Phil watched for approaching cars. He drove carefully to avoid accidents. The street seemed empty, so he backed all the way out. As he was straightening his wheels to start moving forward, he heard an engine's roar. He looked up just in time to see another car bearing down on him.

With the crash, Phil's car was rocked, and he was knocked to the side, across the front seat. Shocked and confused, he slowly rose off the seat. "Are you guys all right?" he asked his passengers. They, too, were starting to sit up. Phil turned to look at the other vehicle in time to see two black kids getting out. They were pointing sawed-off shotguns at him.

Fear rushed from his stomach, through his heart, and struck his mind. All he could think to do was to lie back down on the seat and play dead. He knew that he soon might be. As he slumped to the floor, his eyes passed the car's two-way radio, and he reached for the mike.

I was doing some paperwork in the lieutenants' office when I heard his call on the radio. "Oh, God! Help! Outside the A&P! Two guys with shotguns. They rammed my car!" I couldn't recognize Phil's voice. It had gone up in pitch and whoever it was sounded like they were on the verge of hysteria. As I made my way to the door, the "All available officers to the Control Center" call came over the P.A. system.

I rushed into the Control Center. Warden Wezowicz was

there. He was just finishing an order to the Control Center officer, "Call the police!" I was reaching for the key to the armory when he stopped me.

"Don't let anymore staff go out there." I started to protest that one of our own was in trouble. He saw the look on my face and said, "I'm not sending any of my people out there to be shot."

I knew he was right. We didn't know how many gunmen there were, or where they might be. If we went charging out there they might shoot the officer who had called for help. I called the A&P Room.

The phone rang and rang. Finally, one of the inmate workers answered. He said that the A&P officers had gone out to investigate. There was no other car in sight.

I later learned that the gunmen had looked into Phil's vehicle and checked the passengers. They apparently didn't find the person they were looking for and got back into their car and fled. The car had been stolen and was found later that day. Were they going to free the prisoner or kill him? We never found out.

After that day, no one thought being an unarmed escort officer was a plum job.

Adrenaline High

The TV commercial ended with the idea that no one, as a child, tells their parents that they want to grow up to be a junky. I thought that was a powerful message. But, it also made me realize that kids don't grow up saying, "Mommy, I want to be a correctional officer." Mommy would rush the kid to the nearest shrink. Years after I left the jail system for the relative sanity of the prisons, I posed a question to another training officer, John Roberts. "John, why would anyone go into corrections?"

John thought about it and came up with an interesting answer. "We're all adrenaline junkies," he said. When he said that, I felt an uncomfortable squirming inside. He'd come too close to the truth.

Correctional staff often like to live "on the edge." Life seems so much fuller if you risk losing it. That doesn't mean that any of us enjoy the fights, riots, or the confinement of a hospital bed. But, we get a high from the action in the job. In some correctional staff, this need isn't completely fulfilled by the job. Their hobbies and lifestyles are also filled with danger.

One correctional worker we'll call "Snake" had a need to try to bed every female that he met. There was a Catholic nun who use to come to Seyms Street to help with prayer services. She was an attractive lady, and Snake had his eye on her.

After church services, she would sometimes stop in for a cup of coffee in the staff mess hall. Snake would always manage to be there when that happened. The nun had talked with several staff members and was just rising to leave. Snake came to the table with a cup of coffee and said, "You're not leaving already!" The nun said that she had to go, and walked to the door. Snake's hungry eyes followed her. I said, "God will get you for what you're thinking." Snake said, "I'd like to fuck that!" As the words left his mouth, the hot cup of coffee tipped over into his lap. I was looking at the cup when it fell. No one touched it or the table it was on. It fell for no reason!

Snake had been married several times. We always thought that his desire for "the chase" was the primary reason that he couldn't seem to stay married.

An officer, I'll call him "Sam," took his danger in a similar fashion, with a small twist. Sam was a middle-aged black man, but his specialty was pursuing white women who were usually married.

One night, Sam scored with a woman whose husband worked midnights in some factory. She brought him home to her nice, upper-class, all-white neighborhood. The activities were strenuous and Sam fell asleep. He was awakened by the panicky housewife who said, "Hurry! We overslept! My husband will be walking in any minute."

Sam got dressed and went out the back way. When he was

in the backyard he realized that a black man would be instantly spotted in this lily white neighborhood. Her neighbors might report to her husband if he just walked out into the street. What to do? As he considered his predicament, his eyes fell on a row of garbage cans. He thought, "They must see black garbagemen here all the time." He picked up an empty can and walked to the street with it. Seeing some people on the pavement, he raised it to cover his face, and kept walking. He later said, "I carried that can for four blocks, until I was out of that area."

Correctional staff, like police officers, tend to socialize with their peers. It is hard to go to a party and have someone exclaim, "Oh, you're one of those..." Average people are totally amazed when, during the course of a conversation, they find out that correctional staff don't walk their posts armed. "No, Virginia, we don't even carry a club!" The public doesn't know what we go through. Frankly, it's too much trouble for most of us to educate some limp-wristed liberal who is only going to corrupt our words in the next conversation that he or she has with the news media. That's why, Mr. & Mrs. John Q. Public, your public servants, don't take great pleasure in associating with people outside their professions. Correctional staff, like cops, tend to have their own watering holes for after work recreation.

It's funny how a bar or lounge becomes a "C/O place." Usually there is no mystery to it. They pick the bar that is nearest to their jail. On occasion, they may send out people to look for a new watering hole. This usually happens when (a) they get tired of the same old faces, or (b) when the management makes it known that they are no longer welcome. Scouting parties went out several times in my five years in the Hartford jail system.

One party returned with news of a new hunting ground. It was in the land of East Hartford. We were told that we would not have to ford the mighty Connecticut River as there was a bridge. Our steeds would be well protected by aged security guards who patrolled the parking lot on a regular basis.

The scouts said that the Great Father had blessed these new hunting grounds with bands that would play soothing music, nubile wenches to tend our wounds, and drinks that poured forth at little expense. We mounted up and sallied forth.

On one particular evening, the raiding party consisted of a deputy warden (who left early and missed the fun), two lieutenants (who stayed and were sorry for it), and one officer (who didn't give a shit, before or after). They sat around their table like their ancient warrior counterparts—not passing a peacepipe, just hoisting drinks.

In walked Officer Grant. You'll remember him from his inept handling of the inmates in the Hole. He'd brought a friend. This was another black man, but, unlike Grant, he was not big and powerful. Grant's friend was of average size. He was the type of person who takes satisfaction in using larger friends to protect him from real or imagined snubs.

Friend of Grant (herein known as "FOG") spied a beautiful Hispanic girl dancing with a white man. He walked up to the couple (not knowing if they were married to each other or complete strangers), tapped the guy on the shoulder, and announced, "I'm cutting in!" The couple, who were probably enjoying each other's company said, "No you're not!" and danced away.

FOG, totally unaware that he was not a beautiful creature, was pissed. He handled the rejection like any man of his nature would—he cried to his bigger buddy, Grant. Grant said, "Oh yeah, we'll see about this!" Grant strutted (he never walked) up to the couple. He strutted even more now because he was carrying his .357 magnum, chrome plated, gee-ain't-it-pretty handgun in the shoulder holster under his jacket. He brought his huge paw down on the guy's shoulder, noticing casually that the guy almost went to his knees, and said, "I'm cutting in!"

The poor slob knew he was being attacked. He jumped away from his new-found true love for tonight, and assumed a karate stance. His father had once guaranteed that this move would scare the shit out of anyone. Grant stood there staring at him. It wasn't that he wasn't impressed; it just took five seconds for whatever he saw to register in the three cells that made up his brain (two of which had been killed by alcohol an hour ago).

The little red light exploded its warning in his cranium, "THREAT! THREAT! THREAT!" His bearpaw slid into his jacket and found the .357 magnum (who his father had said was even better than some stupid karate stance). He started to draw it out. White-boy (who wasn't totally stupid and had been propelled forward when he shit in his pants) charged. He must have been slipping in something because his head went down and he hit Grant in the stomach instead of grabbing his arm as he'd intended.

Grant kept going backward. White-boy fell on his face. This knocked him unconscious and for years afterward he probably wondered if he'd been a hero or simply lucky. As luck would have it (Grant's anyway), there was a table with about three hundred glasses stacked on it behind him when he made his move to capture the fair damsel. His two hundred and fifty pounds crashing through a wall of glass attracted some attention. He attracted the attention of about two hundred patrons of the watering hole, two somewhat inebriated lieutenants, one stoned C/O, and about three thousand security guards. Grant did a beautiful roll out of the glass and came up with the .357 in his hand.

As Grant's eyes searched for the person that had caused the alarm bells to go off in his mind (giving him a headache), three correctional staff did a good imitation of Olympic hurdlers breaking records to reach him. Meanwhile, the Public were doing a good impression of a GI digging a foxhole while under mortar fire. Their screams were said to have been heard in Springfield, and registered three on the Richter scale.

The two lieutenants and the C/O hit Grant like a ton of proverbial bricks, and melted to the ground with him. They tried everything in modern police science to wrestle the gun away from him. One of these techniques involves sticking the web of your hand between the hammer and frame of the gun. In theory this prevents the firing pin from striking the cartridge. If the asshole who is trying to shoot you squeezes the trigger, it is also very painful. It imbeds the firing pin into the web of your hand.

So, here we have two lieutenants and one C/O rolling on the ground with someone who weighed as much as any two of them. One of the three was screaming about the gun that was imbedded in his hand, and all three wanted to shoot the fucking scouts that had found this place!

They got the gun away from him. Not only that, none of them died. One lieutenant started to escort Grant out of the place, but was redirected to an office by a very elderly, nervous security guard. He told them that the police were on the way and they'd better not try to leave. Like some of the people in the bar, he would have wet his pants if they had growled at him.

The lieutenant was trying to calm Grant when a voice came from the bar, clear above the moans of wet patrons. "Who the fuck does that nigger think he is, trying to dance with a white girl? Give me a knife and I'll cut off his balls!" This, of course, was said by some wanna-be KKK member as he huddled behind the bar. Grant, having lost his sense of humor, burst from his chair in the office and vaulted a counter.

The security guard dove under a desk and the lieutenant jumped after Grant. The lieutenant caught Grant and decided to get him out of there. As they entered the parking lot, fifteen of East Hartford's finest swooped in and threw both of them against a cruiser. The lieutenant tried to explain and was frisked. Since they found two guns on him (he'd stuck Grant's in his belt after freeing it from the web of the other staff member's hand) he was handcuffed and thrown in the back of a cruiser. They didn't find any weapons on Grant, and didn't handcuff him until the security guard (wiping his pants with a towel) pointed him out.

Both were taken to the East Hartford Police Department.

Grant started fuming about the events in the bar (no doubt his mind had just registered what had happened). He said, "That fucking asshole jumped me! I'll kill the motherfucker when I see him." All this, and more, in front of a scholarly looking police lieutenant. He let Grant rave a while. Then he said, "My father is a minister. I'm not use to that kind of language. If you persist, I'm going to throw you into the fucking jail overnight." Grant's mouth sprung open. There was something wrong with what the lieutenant had said, but he wasn't sure what it was.

He was still trying to figure it out an hour later when they were dumped on the street. Grant had a ticket in his pocket for disorderly conduct and failure to carry his pistol permit, but that didn't bother him as much as what the lieutenant had said. Was his father really a minister? He wondered what church.

Sexual and drinking adventures are just some of the ways that some staff bought an extra dose of danger. Others took more conventional routes. There were a higher than normal amount of staff who were volunteer firemen, rode motorcycles, and I was a part-time police officer (for thirteen years). There was another side to "living on the edge."

In 1981, a national survey of police officers was undertaken. The purpose of this survey was to measure the stress level of those officers by examining factors like heart attacks, ulcers, divorces, drug and alcohol abuse, etc. No one was surprised when the results showed that police officers were among the most stressed of occupational groups.

In 1983, the same parameters were used to measure the stress levels of correctional staff. They found that the incidence of the stress factors in correctional staff was two to three times higher than in the police study. They also found that the life expectancy for people who had spent their careers in corrections was fifty-eight years, compared to seventy years for a white male in the rest of society. In the five years that I was in the jail system, three staff members committed suicide.

Easy Rider

Personal security is vital to every law enforcement officer. This applies to both on-the-job, and off-duty situations. There is nothing that is guaranteed to reduce the coolest, most professional correctional officer to the level of a slavering, homicidal maniac like expressions such as: "Hey man. I know where your wife works (or kids go to school)!" or "I know where you live!" If you want to see police brutality close up and personal, use one of those expressions after Officer Friendly gives you your next traffic ticket.

When, years after Seyms Street, I'd lecture at our academy, I always interspersed my lectures with "Fedorowich's Rules." These were basically war stories that got across some important points to help staff survive. One of the things I did is to have everyone in the class take out their wallets. Then I asked them to go through the cards, pictures, phone numbers, and other forms of information that the wallets held. I instructed them to look at the contents as if they'd just found a stranger's wallet, and see what they could learn about the stranger. As they were doing this, I asked them questions. "Can you tell where this person lives? Can you tell if they have a family? What else can you discover that you wouldn't want an inmate to know?"

It was gratifying to see their looks of surprise and unease. Then I'd tell them that Fedorowich's first rule was: "Leave all personal items outside the jail or prison that you'll be working at in the future." There would usually follow concerns about how they could come to work without their wallets. I'd suggest that they lock them in their vehicles or their lockers.

A recruit once suggested that precautions like that show paranoia. To this I answered that paranoia is a healthy state in law enforcement. I suggested that even if she discounted the monetary loss associated with replacing all the items that stuff our wallets, the emotional trauma associated with murderers, rapists, and child molesters knowing where she and her family lived would be enough reason to take my suggested precaution. Some listened; some didn't want to face the possibilities.

John and Blue were two inmates that were always together, both on the street and in jail. They were burglars. During their latest escapade, they'd broken into a large drugstore through the roof. When an alarm summoned the police, they found themselves with nowhere to go. Not seeing a favorable solution to their problem, they started popping pills from the pharmacy. When the police finally entered, they were both comatose. After their stomachs were pumped they became residents of our little hotel—again.

John and Blue liked to joke with me, but there was an edge to their humor. They didn't like me, and I didn't have any nice feelings about them. On several occasions, I caught them in minor violations like stealing food from the mess hall. I didn't cut them any slack. Their jokes became less humorous and more taunting.

John and Blue had a loose, jail relationship with three other inmates. One of these lived in the same town as I, and I was concerned that he would tell other inmates where I lived. I never knew if he told them, but seeing him with John and Blue made me a little uneasy.

One day, Blue said to me, "Hey Sarge, when me and John get out how about having a little party with us? We'll bring a case of beer to Somers (the town I live in) and party." I said, "Sounds good to me, Blue. When are you two going to start training?" I knew I had him by the perplexed look on his face. "Training? Training for what?" I said, "Training to run faster than the speeding bullets that will be flying at you if I ever see you in my town." He said, "Aw, Sarge, you wouldn't do that. You're not being serious." I told him, "Blue, I'm serious as cancer. Show up near my house and you're dead!" He paled a little, chuckled, and walked off.

About a month later, one of the guys that hung around with John and Blue asked to see me. When he sat down he asked if I knew that Blue had been released today. I didn't know that, but said, "Yeah, so?" He, then, told me that John was supposed to get out in two weeks. Even though my conversation with Blue flashed through my mind I played at being ignorant, and urged him to keep talking.

He told me that John and Blue were planning to get me. Blue was suppose to get a car and a shotgun and meet John when he got out. According to their plan they would wait for me by my exit from the highway and "do an Easy Rider" when I drove by on my motorcycle (an Easy Rider referred to shooting someone off of a motorcycle, as had been done in the movie). I asked several questions of the informant, but he kept insisting that that was all that he knew.

John was released on schedule. I began to come to work by different routes, using different vehicles. I also got pictures of both of them, and warned my wife to be alert for them.

Less than a week later, the same informant came to me, waving a newspaper. "Did you hear the news?" he asked. I hadn't, so I reached for the paper. He held back the paper and said, "After John was released, he met Blue in a bar. They were talking about doing you when another patron at the bar recognized them. He was pissed because they'd sold him a stolen TV a while ago, and he got caught with it. They started cussing and this guy began chasing them around the bar with a pool stick. John ran out to the car, reached under the seat, and came out with the shotgun. The guy ran into a load of double-O-buckshot. John's been arrested." Then he stuck out the folded newspaper for my inspection.

The newspaper just gave the details of the incident (i.e., a bar fight that led to a shooting), not all the details that my informant gave me. I pointed this out, and asked where he had gotten the rest of his information. "I just talked to a guy that was in the police lock-up with John," he said.

When I transferred to the prisons years later, I saw John many times. He would never meet my eyes, nod, or in anyway acknowledge my presence as we passed each other every day. I always looked directly at him, hoping that he'd look too. He never did. We both knew why!

Another Milestone

I took my son to his driving test. He talked more than usual, to hide his nervousness. I hid mine by making sure that he didn't see me peeking while he took his written and road tests. He had studied hard and practiced a lot for these tests. He is a good, safe driver and I had confidence that he would pass. But yet...I worried for him, and hoped he wouldn't have to experience failure in this thing that he wanted so badly. As I sat, trying to read a book and be nonchalant, I thought back to sixteen and a half years ago when I got "The Call."

It was a cold December night. I felt the blahs that seem to arrive every year in the week between Christmas and New Year's. Added to the normal low feeling was concern for my wife. She was due at any second and we'd already had one miscarriage.

I normally drove my van to work, but my wife didn't need her car that night. Our young niece was staying over and my wife would be home. As I rolled down I-91, my thoughts were on her, not the job that I was going toward.

I got off of the highway at the North Main Street exit, and rolled by the buildings and places that I'd seen so often. They, like the routes that other work-bound travelers took, no longer held my interest. The difference between me and the average commuter, however, was that I had entered enemy territory. Like the frontiersmen of old, this meant that I subconsciously increased my awareness of potential dangers. As I stopped for the light at Fishfry Street, or drifted passed the projects, my eyes traced a pattern from the front window to the rearview mirrors—aware of any possible signs of approach.

When I reached the jail, my thoughts returned to my wife for the last time, I felt, until the ride home. I trudged up the marble steps and stood in front of the sallyport gate, waiting for the Control Center officer to have a moment to let me in to my work-world.

Lieutenant Barton held roll call. Amid light bantering, and some moaning over their assignments, the officers moved to their posts. A night like any other.

The inmates were released, a block at a time, for the evening meal. As I was locking the lieutenants' office, the door leading to the main corridor crashed open. I heard Officer Jerry Hall yell, "Get in here, now!" Inmate Sweet sauntered in to the waiting area. His whole body spoke of the belligerence he felt. "You got no reason to talk to me like that. I'm a man! Don't treat me like one of your kids. You want to talk to your kids, go home," he shouted as he came within inches of Jerry's face.

In the instant before I spoke I remembered my two previous encounters with Sweet. On one occasion, I walked up on him as he was talking to Billy Lynch. Billy was turned at a ninety degree angle away from Sweet. His body language told me that he didn't have time for this and would rather be somewhere else. Billy was chewing on his toothpick. His head was tilted down, as if he was listening intently.

As Sweet whined about his ill treatment at the hands of a "white-honky officer," Billy (like a preacher in a Baptist revival) kept saying, "You're right! You're right!" Unlike that preacher, when Billy said it, the meaning came out, "You're full of shit! You're full of shit!" The crowd around the two, listened. Their heads went back and forth as if they were watching a tennis match. Such was the respect that they held for Billy that after each realized what he was really saying to Sweet, they wandered off, shaking their heads in disgust.

The other time I met Sweet I was in our infirmary. Sweet came in and immediately started to whine, to Medic Pete Ivory, about how no one was taking his "foot problem" seriously. Pete had been a Navy medic. He'd seen about every medical condition that organization could produce. His attitude toward Sweet told me that he wasn't finished with goldbrickers when he left the Navy. "What's the problem?' he asked, as Sweet sat on the examining table and undid his size thirteen shoes. "I got bunions, corns, and warts. My arches is falling and I think I'm getting athletes foot," said Sweet.

As his feet were uncased from their apparently airproof shoes, I had to step back or throw up. Pete didn't even blink. "I suppose they're making you work, on top of everything else?" he asked. "Yeah, they want me to mop floors and everything. When my feet gets wet, they gets worse," whined Sweet. Pete was the epitome of concern as he said, "You've got to get your feet wet, but this time you'll use soap. I want you to come here three times a day to wash and soak your feet." Sweet said, "Okay, Boss. Can I have a pass that says I don't have to work?" Pete said, "No. You come between work hours." Sweet left, not totally unhappy. The pass would allow him to leave his block three times a day, wander around, and eventually get to the hospital.

As my thoughts returned from these experiences with

Sweet, I asked Jerry what had happened. Jerry said, "I'll take care of this, Sarge." His lack of answer, and disregard of my authority might have bothered me in other circumstances, but I remembered Jerry from Somers. I knew he was a good officer. I was somewhat taken aback by what happened next.

Both Jerry and Sweet were black men of the same build, but Sweet was a head taller and a lot more verbally aggressive than Jerry. Jerry grabbed the front of Sweet's shirt and pushed him against the wall. I could hear the crowd passing by the screened door come to a stop. They began to murmur. Jerry said, "Every time I ask you to do something you give me a ration of shit. I'm fed up with you! Nobody calls me a fucking Uncle Tom. I'm tired of you and your threats! You want to do something? Do it now! You ain't no murderer. You're a slimy purse snatcher. Take your best shot!" Sweet stood there, shaking in anger. The crowd behind the screened door restlessly shouted, "Hit him, Sweet! Don't let him talk to you like that!" Sweet stood there and, other than shaking, didn't move. Jerry said, "Get the fuck out of my sight. You mess with me again and I'm going to step on your big, ugly feet!"
Sweet slid along the wall until he was out of Jerry's reach. Then he quickly bolted for the door among the catcalls of the other inmates.
I turned to Jerry. He was coming down off of his anger and seemed to realize that he had threatened an inmate in front of a supervisor. I said, "Nice job! Go get a coffee."
As I stepped into the hallway, I looked to the left at the mass of inmates going to eat from the East Wing. Toward the rear of the line I saw three inmates who were walking kind of funny. They looked like they had just come off of a long horseback ride. All three were in pain, but refused to admit it when I confronted them. Each pushed my inquiry aside by attributing their strange way of walking to "hemorrhoids." Later, when I had the chance to talk to one of my snitches in private, I asked about the three inmates.
This man was an older inmate. I think he gave me selected

information that would lead to the downfall of his competitors in one or more of the scams he was always involved in. When I mentioned the three inmates by name, he started to laugh, "They got their come-uppance! They surely did!" I waited for him to go on.

"There's this young white officer—I'm not telling names or shift—that was trying to get those young bucks to toe the line. Well, they weren't about to let him tell them what to do. The other day they cornered him on the top of the Boundover Block. They told him to back off or they'd throw him off of the fucking third tier. The way I heard it, he didn't say much—in a corner like he was. One of my buddies says he saw that officer the next day. All the inmates were disrespecting him because those three had talked about how he'd backed down instead of fighting. This friend of mine says he saw the officer in one of their cells when they were out to recreation. He says that the officer was spraying the toilet paper in the cell with Mace. Now I don't know if that's true or not, but those boys have sure eased up on pushing the other inmates around." I didn't pursue the subject any further.

My night went on like that. One incident led to another, not giving me time to think about the "home front." Jim Barton and I were discussing a disciplinary report (DR) at about eleven o'clock when the phone rang. I picked it up and answered, "Hartford Correctional Center. Sergeant Fedorowich." A faint, scared voice pierced my ear, "Ed, you better come home. My water just broke!" After asking her condition and receiving reassurances, I got permission to leave.

As I screeched out of the parking lot, my foot on the gas pedal never left the floor. I remembered the many times when I'd stopped speeders, in my part-time police work, who were agitated and told of their rush to one emergency or another. I'd always take a moment to slow myself and them down by saying, "Sir (or Madam), THINK! Are you going to be of help to your loved one if you're wrapped around a tree? Get there in good shape so that you can help!" Somehow that advice doesn't apply when it's your emergency. Normally, the ride from the jail to home took about forty minutes. I made it in twenty-five.

As I tore into the driveway, my friends, Dave and Barbara Kenny, were taking our niece to their car. They explained that they would have her sleep at their house and would contact her parents, to pick her up, tomorrow. They were so *calm*. My wife was standing at the door. She had a valise in her hand and a blanket was between her legs, held by the other hand. She explained that she was still "leaking."

While she waddled to the truck, Dave, Barbara, and I closed up the house. Dave was concerned with my mental state. He offered to drive. I turned down his offer, bragging that I was okay. I reminded him that I was a police officer and an EMT. I could handle it!

Boy, did that sound stupid about two seconds after I said it.

Dave took me back inside and said, "Don't forget that you're not going to do her or anyone else any good by wrapping yourself around a tree." He was a part-time cop, too. Then, to calm me down, he said, "You got anything to drink?"

After downing a shot of Old Rotgut, I have to admit that I'd slowed down. I got into my truck next to the girl I'd done this to, and asked, "Are you comfortable?" Thankfully, she was preoccupied with other thoughts or she might have explained how comfortable she was after carrying a hundred pound kid around for nine months. Now the little SOB was pissing down her leg. Instead of that diatribe, she turned to me and said, "I'm okay! Just take it easy to the hospital. Okay?"

I pushed back the urge to tell her that I was a police officer and a trained EMT, and sedately drove toward the hospital, in Hartford. We had taken classes on natural child birth at this hospital. Unfortunately, they were given by people who didn't know what the hell they were talking about. Oh, they may have gotten the birth part right, but the part that the father goes through was written by someone who didn't work there. They said that the father would be brought to a side room to change into an operating room gown, so he could immediately be with his wife. Instead, they directed me to a waiting room populated by androids that smoked, watched TV, and read, like they were waiting for a splinter to be removed from their wives' fingers.

One fool even looked at his watch and said, "Christ, two hours! Hey, Nurse, I've got to go to work in the morning. Tell my wife to call me when it's over. I'll have to get someone to watch the other three when I come to visit."

All this time, I'm standing outside the waiting room. I'm waiting for someone to bring me to that room where I can change and return to my wife's side. I was beginning to feel like a hitchhiker on the side of a highway. "Nurse, when can I...Don't run off! Doctor. Oh, you're not a doctor. You handle the bed pans? Well, maybe you can help me...Don't run off!"

After three hundred hours (more or less), a nurse came to the door and said, "Mr. Feda...Feda." I said, "That's me!" tripped over some asshole's feet, and almost landed on top of the nurse. I could just imagine what would happen if I'd knocked her out. I'd never find my wife in the maze of corridors. She led me to the promised room and helped me put on the head piece, gown, and booties. During the next several hours, I watched staff members of the hospital, who were wearing none of these things, come into my wife's room to provide various types of attention to her. I finally figured that they dressed the husbands that way so they could tell who the jerk was, and not confuse him with some hyperactive doctor.

My wife went through hours of hell which no humor could lighten or shorten. The breathing exercises helped in only a marginal way. The kid did not want to come out! He must have known what our world is like.

Finally, her doctor drew me outside. He looked at me with basset hound eyes and said, "Your wife is in a lot of pain." I was torn between smacking him or being sarcastic. Just in time, I remembered that this wizard might be in a position to decide my wife's and/or child's fate. I controlled myself and asked what he suggested. In medical terms he said, "Let's knock her out!"

After I'd agreed to this, and the drug had been administered, a nurse approached me, "Mr. Feda...Feda..." I said, "That's me!" I wondered how nurses could pronounce Señor Juan Garcia Fidalgo's name (with proper inflection and dialect) and never seem to get passed the first syllable of my name. Must be a course in nursing school. Anyway, she asked me to follow her. I protested that I wanted to stay with my wife. "Look, I've even got on the suit."

"*It's against hospital policy!*" she said with accompanying nasal inflection. At a loss for what to do next, I had a brilliant thought and whipped out my badge, as if to say, "I can take it!" She looked at the bright silver as if I was a little boy who had whipped out his peepee, and said, "Very nice. This way, please."

She watched as I disrobed—well the hospital stuff, anyway. Then she escorted me back to the android waiting room. Before I'd let her go, I made her swear on her mother that she would return every fifteen minutes to let me have a report on my wife. She fooled me! She didn't have a mother!

After 3,742 laps of the room (rumor was that they had snipers who would shoot if you stepped out the door) the same doctor who had tricked me into leaving my wife's side entered. He had a stack of papers in his hand that he wanted me to sign. By this time, I was ready to say, "Look, Doc, I don't care if she has an heir to the Fedorowich name. No one can pronounce the name anyway. Just give my wife back to me!" He informed me that he was going to try, one more time to use forceps to pull the child out. If that didn't work, they would have to do a cesarean section. I signed everything without reading it. I may have even reenlisted in the service for all I knew. I just pleaded that they save my wife! He promised that he'd let me know what happened as soon as he could.

Hours and hours went by! Each nurse I asked either admitted ignorance of my wife's condition or said something like, "I'm from geriatrics." Finally, the doctor returned. I looked at his somber demeanor and almost slobbered, "My wife, Doc? How is she?" He looked at me like he'd discovered a new leper in his colony and said, "Mr. Feda...Feda...?" I almost yelled, "That's me! What can you tell me? My wife?"

He said, "Oh, didn't anyone tell you?" I looked over his shoulder, expecting to see the hospital's chaplain.

"No," I said. "Your wife had a boy. Both are fine!"

I stopped by the recovery room long enough to kiss my wife, promise her I'd be back at visiting hours, and make her admit that I'd been right about our child's sex. Then I went down to the observation room. The nurses there were so busy that they didn't have time to hold up my bit of immortality, so I took a guess as to which he was and left.

A newly-purchased fifth of Old Rotgut and I arrived home. While sampling its contents, I called everyone in the world.

I went to bed and got up in time to visit my wife and hold my son for the first time.

"We Wish You
A Merry Christmas..."

Holidays are a sad time for those who are forced to be away from home. Christmas seems to be the hardest. This isn't to imply that I had a lot of sympathy for the inmates. Most of them were in their "home" or, at least, had some control over what they did and where they spent Christmas. If you work in corrections, you know that it can be a period of emotion, sadness, and suicide.

Staff wants to be home on Christmas, too. Supervisors try to give as many officers the day off as possible. Officers who were not lucky enough to have a day off granted to them will try other means, but there is an unwritten rule that no one calls in sick on that day. Correction officer mothers and fathers will sometimes find a single staff member who will trade a

Christmas Day or Eve for a New Year's Day or Eve.

Everyone makes plans, and it is left to those who work to try to balance security needs with showing some humanity toward the inmates. There were always extra church services, special meals, and other amenities that the staff had to handle with less than enough people.

On my first Christmas in the jail, I was the lowest seniority supervisor, and so was scheduled to work the 4–12 shift. It was to be one of my first nights alone and in charge.

The shift ran smoothly, thanks to the seasoned staff, until it came time for lock-up. I received word that something was going on in the East Wing. Officers reported seeing inmates gathering in groups in the bullpen. It was too quiet, even for Christmas.

When the officers gave the call to lock up on the bullhorn, none of the inmates obeyed. They continued to play cards, watch TV, or just talk in their groups. When I arrived on the scene, I told the officers to send the sentenced, inmate workers back to their blocks and to shut off the TV.

The East Wing inmates were all unsentenced. They knew that they would soon go to court. Their case might be thrown out for one reason or another, they might make bail, or they might be sentenced and go to Somers. They knew they wouldn't be in jail long, and that it would be difficult for us to impose sanctions on them for unacceptable behavior. Consequently, they didn't listen to orders when they didn't want to.

I tried talking with some of the inmates who were gathered about to find out why they weren't locking up. Most wouldn't talk, but one who did said they wanted to "wait up until Santa Claus gets here." Others shouted from the bullpen, "Hey, Sarge. It's Christmas. Give us a break!"

I knew that to yield to their request would be the same as letting them run the jail. I tried talking to them with the bullhorn: "Okay. You've had your fun. Now it's time to lock up before you bite off a bigger piece than you can chew." Their replies varied from an uncertained silence to, "Chew this! You fucking Scrooge!" When they'd quieted, I had the officers go and prepare to lock up anyone who wanted to go in. Several did, amongst the catcalls of the others. The rest refused.

As they left me with no option, I started dialing numbers from the emergency call-in list. Within half an hour, off-duty staff began to arrive. Some of the lieutenants and captains tried to talk some sense into the inmates. They had no effect.

As some officers began to report that they'd gotten word that the inmates were beginning to arm themselves with makeshift weapons, the administrators decided to equip the officers with riot gear. At about eleven thirty at night, we felt we had enough staff to go in and lock them up by force.

Officers Sebbie Cardella and Ramon Martinez, wearing riot gear, joined me by the officers' desk as I, again, reached for the bullhorn. The other riot-equipped officers were hiding, out of sight of the inmates. I announced, "You will return to your cells immediately. Anyone who fails to comply with this order may be subject to having force used on them." The cell doors were opened, but no one moved. The inmates were enjoying the fact that they'd ruined part of the Christmas for some of the staff.

Suddenly, from the group of thirty hidden officers, came singing. I didn't recognize the song at first because it was sung like a funeral dirge. As their footsteps clanged against the metal steps, I heard, "We wish you a Merry Christmas. We wish you a Merry Christmas…" Inmates started to move toward their cells. Soon there was a rush to get their cell doors locked before the pissed-off officers (with clubs) reached them.

Feeling contempt for the inmates and being flushed with the ease of our battle, I picked up the bullhorn and said, "Bah humbug!"

Suicide

Of all the stupid, wasteful things that mankind does to itself, suicide has to be up near the top of God's Top Ten List. Because the individual cannot deal with some aspect, or even all of his life, he takes it upon himself to decide that his parents will be without their child, his wife her husband, and his children their father.

In any jail system, the staff will see suicide attempts that range from a pitiful cry for help to a deliberate, well planned success. Each must be considered to be a serious attempt, and the inmate must receive psychiatric help.

At Seyms Street I witnessed many attempted suicides. The methods used varied from diving from the third or fourth tier, to swallowing pills or cleaning supplies, to cutting one's wrist, to the most popular—hanging. Hangings became so frequent that we even had inmate janitors (called "tiermen") watching for them.

The tiermen were sentenced inmates who could receive "good time." Good time is a shortening of an inmate's sentence because he had all-around good conduct or he did some heroic deed. Inmates must be nominated for good time by a staff member.

When the jail staff became nervous about the frequency of attempted suicides and passed on their concern to the tiermen, one of these enterprising individuals got an idea. He decided to become the most diligent suicide spotter in the jail.

In short order, he became a hero. He discovered three attempted suicides in just one week. Of course he was nominated for good time on each occasion, just like he'd planned.

It wasn't until later that we realized that we'd been scammed. Our "hero" had approached each of the potential victims. He'd explained that if they'd pretend to attempt suicide they would be moved to the hospital wing where they'd have better treatment and could score drugs. They would also be helping him out because he would find them in the act, save them, and get the good time.

The only reason we caught on to this tierman's scam was that another tierman tried the same thing with fires. He would set a fire, leave the area, and return in time to "discover" it and raise an alarm. We became suspicious and stopped awarding good time for finding fires. Strangely, the fires stopped. Then we stopped submitting names for good time for finding suicide attempts and these just about stopped.

Of course, all attempts weren't the result of enterprising plans. Some were very, very real.

Inmate John Jordan was a quiet, respectful person. He was a twenty-year-old black man who had never been arrested before. He came from a respectable, upper-middle-class family, and was very sad when he thought about the dishonor that he had brought to them. John was guilty of the crime, but couldn't deal with having been caught. John was a child molester.

Child molesters are hated by all inmates. Inmates, especially those with children of their own, will go out of their way to do something to hurt a "baby ripper." John had been in several scuffles since the word had leaked out about his crime. It was thought to be wise to put him in administrative segregation until he was either sentenced by the court or found not guilty and released.

Administrative segregation inmates were housed in the Northwest Wing. They were allowed all the privileges of regular inmates except that they ate and had recreation in the Northwest Wing. They had no contact with inmates from the general population.

John paced in his cell while he read the copy of the Bible that the jail's chaplain had sent him. Finding no answers in this book, he gently laid it aside and sat on his bunk. Because he and all of the "seg" inmates were in single cells, he didn't have a cellmate to talk to. He did have Old Man Jenkins in the next cell.

"Old Man Jenkins," was how his neighbor had introduced himself when John was first brought to seg. Everyone referred to him by that name, but over time, John started to call him "Jenks," and the old man didn't seem to mind.

"Jenks, are you ever sorry for what you did to get in here?"

Jenkins put down the girlie magazine he was "reading" and said, "Boy, you got to let it go. You be reading that Bible and trying to find answers, but there ain't no answers for us. We going to do time! Get used to it and stop worrying yourself about being sorry. I been coming to jail since before you were born. I don't feel sorry for no one. I only sorry that I get caught!"

"But, did you ever hurt anyone when you did your crimes?"

"Well, I suppose it depends on what you mean by 'hurt.' I steal things. I steal from houses and businesses. Once a guy walked in on me and I had to knock him out. Put him in the hospital! But that was his fault for trying to stop me. You hurt someone?"

"Yeah, I guess I did."

"Don't worry! After you spend some time here you won't think about it much."

But John did think about it. More importantly, to him, he thought about his parents. How are they dealing with this? If he hadn't got caught...but, he did get caught. Now they know!

At this point the block officer opened John's celldoor and announced, "Shower time." John gathered his cosmetics and toilet items and walked to the shower at the end of the tier. As always, he was very scrupulous about cleanliness. He finished showering and returned to his cell.

As the evening went on, other inmates were released for showers or declined when their time came. John stared at the ceiling and drew further into himself. The officer made his rounds, checking on everyone. After he passed John's cell, John got up and took his sheet off of his bed. He knew that the officer wouldn't be back for another half hour, if then. He had all the time in the world.

John carefully knotted the sheet to the top bar of his cell. Standing with his back to the bars, he tightened the sheet around his neck and made a slipknot. He closed his eyes and without making a sound, bent his knees, letting the noose take the full weight of his body. As the noose tightened around his throat he almost panicked and jumped to his feet. But the blood stopped flowing to his brain and he quickly passed from a conscious state to death.

About fifteen minutes later, Old Man Jenkins felt the urge to go to the toilet. It was then that he realized that he'd forgotten to get a roll of toilet paper when he was out for his shower. Cursing the onset of his apparent senility he said, "Hey, boy, you got any toilet paper? I run out." Getting no answer after repeated attempts, he called to the officer, "Hey, Officer, can you bring a roll of toilet paper up to Old Man Jenkins? I got to shit real bad and I ran out."

Various inmate voices suggested that he use his sheets or not bother to wipe because he smelled like shit anyway. "The hell with you guys. How about it, Officer?" The block officer wearily replied, "Okay. I'm coming!"

The block officer's tired boredom instantly disappeared when he reached John's cell. After he got over the disbelief, he yelled down to the other officer on duty and ran to the end of the tier to release the deadlock bar. When he got the cell opened, he grabbed John around the waist and raised him to take the pressure off of his neck. As other staff arrived they attempted to loosen the sheet that had imbedded itself into his flesh. Finally, one officer was able to carefully cut the cloth with a pocket knife.

I shouted above the turmoil, "Bring him to the end of the tier so we'll have room to work on him." Once this was done, I checked his vital signs. No pulse! No breathing! Pupils dilated and non-responsive to light! "He's dead," I said. Just then, Lieutenant Brown arrived. I explained that it was no use, but the lieutenant said, "We've got to try to save him. Let's start CPR."

This was in the days before there were protective devices to help prevent the spread of disease during mouth-to-mouth breathing. None of us knew this inmate or what diseases he might have. When Lieutenant Brown made that statement, all the officers started to find something interesting to look at on the ceiling. I was relatively new to the jail and wanted to make a good impression (but I wasn't stupid). "I've got the chest," I said as I started to do compressions.

"Who'll volunteer for the mouth?" the lieutenant asked. Total silence! Finally, seeing that he'd get no volunteers, the lieutenant said, "You guys have no guts. I'll do it!"

As I was doing the chest compressions and the lieutenant was breathing for the inmate, I noticed that the inmate's stomach was becoming more and more distended with each breath. I knew what that meant and said, "Dave, this guy's going to barf." Lieutenant Brown, between breaths, said, "What?" Just as he says this, the "golden rainbow" appeared.

The lieutenant got a mouthful of vomitus and the rest of us jumped back as both the lieutenant and the dead inmate sprayed the area.

Medic Pedigrew arrived, cleared the inmate's mouth, and began providing respirations with a bagmask. We kept this up all the way to the hospital where Inmate John Jordan was pronounced "dead on arrival."

Oddballs

The reader may think that it is strange to see a chapter entitled "Oddballs" when this book is about people who the average John Q. Public would consider different or "oddball." In defining the term, I felt that it applied to folks whose thought processes led them to believe that the things that are important in life are not the same things that I (or any average person) would feel the same way about. The term "oddball" is not meant to be derogatory, but, rather, different.

Jacob was a twenty-six-year-old black man. He'd been incarcerated at Seyms Street several times before this entombment. In each of his past sentences (which were for relatively minor offenses), he had attended the weekly Protestant

services. His voice could be heard above all of the congrega-
tion when it came time to sing hymns or utter prayers. His
behavior outside of church was of a penitent who realized that
he had done wrong. He seemed to be searching for help.

On this incarceration, however, he'd been brought in like
a mad dog. Two police officers had escorted him as he made
his way from the patrol car. He was in handcuffs and leg irons.
The police did not normally use leg irons unless they were
dealing with a problem case. Jacob was shouting, snarling,
and barking as they brought him into the jail.

Because of our past knowledge of him, and his present
behavior, we deemed it wise to put Jacob into a cell in the
hospital wing. In a few days he had changed back to the Jacob
we knew.

One day an officer searched Jacob's cell. He came to me
with a handful of chicken bones and a puzzled expression on
his face. "I found these in Jacob's cell," he said. "Are they
contraband?"

Contraband was described as anything an inmate had that
(1) had not been issued to him, (2) he had not purchased in the
commissary, or (3) had been altered from its original condition. The officer was confused because chicken is given to the
inmates in the mess hall. I told him that it should be treated as
contraband, just as a chicken sandwich that had been smuggled
out of the mess hall would be considered contraband. The
only difference was in the particular part of the chicken that
had been stolen. He nodded his understanding and went off
to write a disciplinary report on Jacob for theft and a sanitary
violation.

Later, as part of the procedure for issuing the disciplinary
report, I interviewed Jacob. "Sergeant," he exclaimed, "give
my bones back." I explained that he couldn't take any part of
the food that he was given in the mess hall back to his cell.
This included bones.

He was very agitated, and could hardly wait for me to stop
talking before he said, "But you don't understand. Them's
religious bones!" I said, "Jacob, I know you go to church a lot,

but I don't remember anything in the Protestant religion that entails bones."

"No. No," he said, " It ain't nothing to done with Protestants. This is my religion!" I asked what religion he was talking about. He said, "Don't have a name, but's what I believe."

All law enforcement officers are aware of the Constitution. No one wants to be sued for violating an individual's right to pursue his religious beliefs. I couldn't allow him to keep his "bones" in his cell because any inmate would then be able to say that the contraband he had was "part of his religious beliefs."

I questioned Jacob some more. He believed that by throwing his bones, and reading them, he could determine what his future behavior should be. He wouldn't listen to any suggestion that his bones weren't holy or that he should speak to a chaplain. His bones told him what was right!

I'd known Jacob's mother from past telephone conversations. She'd always told me, "If my son gets into some kind of trouble when he's with you, call me and I'll set him straight. He's a good boy." I pulled his file, and dialed his mother's number. As I listened to the dial tone, I read a note from his file. It said, "Subject should be watched, as he may be a danger to himself. He killed his mother by beating her with the thigh bone of a cow."

Ivan believed in the United States Constitution. He believed that nothing that was not granted to the states or to the federal government in the Constitution was within their control. He believed that no local zoning official had any authority over his property, nor did any judge have the right to put him into jail.

Ivan was brought into Seyms Street Jail by two burly sheriffs who deposited him on a bench with a thud. Ivan took pains to explain to the receiving officer that he had been kidnapped by two criminals when he was in court. He implored the correctional officer to set him free, and not be part of this "kidnapping." The officer, diligently, called me. "We've got a flake," he said.

I went to the A&P, unsure as to what I'd find. The officer nodded to a little old man who was sitting on a bench in the receiving area. He unlocked the door and I entered. I started my conversation with Ivan by asking him if he knew why he was here. He said, "Of course I do! I've been kidnapped." I explained that he'd been brought here on legitimate court papers, which I'd already examined. He said, "But you don't understand. That person who calls himself a judge has no right to incarcerate me." He further warned that if I didn't release him immediately, I would be a conspirator in his kidnapping. Having just completed a course on Constitutional law, I tried to convince him that the judge had the right to lock his ass up. After a half-hour, I gave up. The question now was whether he would comply with the institutional rules or not.

I explained that although I could empathize with his position, he was going to spend some time in our little motel. Would he obey our rules? He calmly stated that he had been kidnapped and could not morally comply with the orders of his kidnappers. I asked, "If I tell you to strip, as part of the admittance process, does that mean that you are going to fight with us?" He thought about his answer for a moment, and said, "I am a frail old man. I cannot fight you if you insist on breaking the law, but I will not in any way help you."

I had to admire the old shit. He was dignified, and his rationale made some sense, but I had a jail to run. I wondered why I felt like a defendant at the Nuremberg Trials. I could hear myself saying, "But, I only obeyed orders." I shook that feeling off and summoned a couple of officers that were standing outside the door.

I explained to them that Ivan was not going to fight us, but that he was not going to help us, either.

I turned to Ivan and said, "Sir, as part of our admittance procedure, you must be strip-searched to ensure that you are not carrying any weapons, drugs, or other contraband. Do you understand this?" He thought a second and asked, "Other than drugs or weapons, what else could I be carrying that you'd be worried about?" I said, "You could, for instance, have a handcuff key hidden in your clothing. Will you act like a man and take your clothes off?"

He looked at me and smiled, "A man doesn't take his clothing off for another man. If you must violate me, go ahead." Feeling like a pervert, I undid the buttons of his shirt, and removed it. Then I took his undershirt off. He sagged back against the cold wall.

One of the officers undid his shoes and removed his socks. I unbuckled his belt, and unzipped his fly. I explained that since he wasn't cooperating an officer and I would have to lift him while his pants were removed. He didn't respond, and we lifted him. After his pants and undershorts were removed, he sat there, stoically. Suddenly, he slipped to the floor. His back was slightly scratched from contact with the bench. He looked at me with anger boiling in his eyes, and said, "I'll sue you for this!"

I turned from him in disgust. When I reached the door, I looked at him and said, "You had me going, for a minute. I could see the logic in your claims. I, too, believe in less government, but you've just proved that you're a lower scumbag than some of our junkies. They can't help themselves while you go out of your way to be scum and pretend to have higher ideals."

I felt pretty good about putting him and his supposedly high ideals down in front of others. We had taken extra care with him. We understood that, in effect, he was being jailed because he had very high ideals regarding the rights of people. In the end, he showed himself to be a lower form of life—one that would take our kindnesses and use them to create a situation where he'd appear to be a martyr. I felt good until I received the court papers that told me he was suing me for $125,000. Then I only felt anger toward false gods and my own idealism.

• • •

Alexander was a tall, thin man. The smell of fear was on him every time we met. If hatred has a smell, it was there too. In every encounter in which I met him, he was ready to fight us. He must have known that we were not going to commit ourselves to battles that we could not win. We would always summon more help, while trying to talk him into compliance. He never budged.

Alexander felt that he was an important part of the Black Liberation Army (BLA). Informers that I spoke with knew of him in a vague way. They couldn't recall anything of revolutionary importance that he'd accomplished while he was "on the streets." Yet, he maintained an attitude of arrogance and hatred toward all whites. He was so good at this that he began to develop a following within the prison walls. That made him a very dangerous person.

One evening when Alexander returned from court, I received a phone call. The A&P Officer said, "That asshole Alexander just came back from court. He won't strip again." I gathered some officers up and went to the A&P Room.

Alexander was all alone in the processing area. He sat with his elbows on his knees, head hanging down. As I approached, he stood and flared his chest. Hatred poured from his eyes. "Look, Alexander, You've been going to court every day. Each night you come back here and refuse to strip. Then we have to fight with you. I'm getting too old for this fighting shit. Why don't you just strip?"

Alexander said, "Do what you have to." I looked at the six other officers there and thought that this fool was really stupid. Every night he'd fight. Every night we'd win. What was the sense in all of it? The only victory that he'd ever had was when one of my officers would pull a back muscle or sprain an ankle while beating the shit out of him.

One of the black officers had been watching this exchange. He said, "Sarge, can I talk to you?" I left Alexander in the care of the other officers and moved to the side. "Sarge, this guy's a mental case," the officer said. "He gets off on being beaten up." I didn't understand. "Sarge, this guy comes when we beat on him."

I knew what he meant then, but didn't quite believe that there were people like that. I knew we'd have to take him to the Hole after fighting with him. If we carried him we'd pass by inmates who'd relay the fact that Alexander wasn't the big fighter that he'd been claiming. When that happened, however, I didn't want a lot of officers to be carrying him. If there were, he'd spend days telling the other inmates that it "took six of the motherfuckers to take him and put him in the Hole."

After I'd talked with the other officer, we returned to Alexander. We had a plan. Alexander was standing with his back to the wall. While talking, I moved toward his right side. The officer moved toward his left. After I tried to convince him to comply for a few more minutes, I grabbed his right arm with my left hand. At the same time, his left arm was pinned by the officer. I brought my left hand to his throat and squeezed his carotid arteries between my thumb and forefinger. He struggled for a second, and became limp.

After we'd strip-searched him, I told one of the officers to get the cart that we used to carry the garbage to the garbage room. We loaded Alexander onto it and wheeled him to the Hole. We passed inmates who could be heard to murmur, "Look at that big hero. He ain't shit! They're taking him out with the other trash."

Some legends die so easily! When we got him into the Hole and on a bunk, he began to wake up. We locked the door as he roared, "You bastards. Come back and fight!"

Crazy As A "Foxie"

Foxie contributed nothing to our society. He held no job, paid no taxes, and supported only himself. Foxie was a pimp! I often wondered how he came into that profession since he was so ugly. One day I asked him.

He said, "Sarge, I followed my heroes." Seeing my confused look, he explained, "Who do you think the heroes are in the ghetto? They're not the working slobs who barely have enough left at the end of the week to buy themselves a beer. They're not the cops. The ones I admired when I was a little kid were the pimps. They had the fancy cars and clothes. They had the beautiful women!"

Foxie was a tall, thin black man. He wasn't just a normal

thin. His knees, elbows, and other joints were so big and knobby that they made him look even more like a skeleton than he really was. He wore his receding hairline slicked down and well greased. His face was so pockmarked that it looked like someone had used it as a dart board.

One visiting day, one of Foxie's "ladies" came to see him. The officers would not let her enter the visiting area because all that she was wearing under her coat was panties, shoes, and a clear plastic dress.

When she was refused entry, she insisted upon seeing a supervisor. Sergeant Jeff Schoenfeldt had a little trouble concentrating on what he was saying while she stood there with a brazen little smile on her face, but he finally got her to leave. When Foxie was called to the office to be told why she couldn't visit, he put on an innocent, surprised expression. He didn't really care whether or not she got in because his bets with the other inmates were that he could get her to come to the jail dressed like that. After the initial explanations were completed he only wanted to know if she had left him any money.

Foxie visited Seyms Street several times in the three years that I was there. His unplanned sabbaticals were usually the result of "disciplining" his girls or a turf war with another pimp. The last time that I saw him was a little different.

One of Foxie's girls was holding out on him. Instead of turning over her earnings, she was saving some, hoping to get enough to break with him and her way of life. Foxie suspected what she was doing, did some checking, and went looking for her. When he caught up to her and told her to get in his car, she ran. By the time Foxie got his Caddy turned around, she had made it to a gas station. She hid in the Ladies Room. Foxie asked some of the people on the street if they'd seen her pass by. One little urchin gave her up.

The bathrooms in the gas station didn't have locking doors. The manager was tired of the junkies locking themselves in so that they could shoot-up in privacy.

Foxie's girl put all of her weight against the door and pushed against the far wall with one foot. She had to pull her skintight dress up to her waist so she could raise her leg high enough. She was sobbing in fear, but tried to muffle her sounds in case he was near.

She jumped and almost fell to the floor when Foxie pounded on the door, shouting her name. As he steadily pressed against the door, she felt it starting to move. Her high heels slipped on the slimy wall, despite her efforts. She began to scream.

Foxie got the door opened wide enough to get his scrawny arm inside. He felt around until he found her hair. Grabbing a handful, he began to bang her head against the door. Her screams drew the manager to the scene. He peeked around the corner, saw enough to decide his wife was right about retirement, and made a dash for the telephone. Foxie's girl was getting weaker. Her foot began to slip down the wall. Finally the door opened wide enough so that he could get his head and other arm inside. As a last, desperate move, she grabbed his other hand and sank her teeth into it. As she felt the warm blood fill her mouth, Foxie's screams were added to hers.

When the police arrived, Foxie was wrapping a silk handkerchief around his hand. The girl wasn't screaming anymore because Foxie had bashed in her nose and teeth trying to get his hand free. He'd taken the time to drop an ugly looking knife next to her unconscious body as the sirens approached.

Foxie told the officers that she'd approached him to sell him sex. When he'd gotten out of the car, she'd tried to hold him up. He'd tried to take the knife away from her, but had been bitten in the process. He struck her, he said, in self-defense.

They knew Foxie, and didn't believe him. As he was loaded into the cruiser, the paramedics arrived.

Foxie had several meetings with his attorney. He was told that the prosecutor wasn't going to let him "slide" on this one. Foxie started to get very worried.

• • •

Medic Ivory called me. He said, "Sarge, come down to the hospital. I've got something that you've got to see." When I tried to press him to find out what the problem was, he said, "You won't believe it until you see it." When I got to the infirmary, Pete indicated one of the cells that was reserved for psychiatric patients.

As I approached it, the smell hit me. "What the hell stinks?" Pete just continued to gesture toward the cell, with a big smile on his face. He patted me on the shoulder and said, "What do we do now, Oh Great Leader? Or rather, What are you going to do now? I don't want any part of this!"

I looked in the cell. There was Foxie, sitting on the floor next to the toilet bowl. He was grinning and mumbling to himself. He had smeared excrement on the cell's walls. I said, "Foxie, what the hell do you think you're doing?" He looked at me and held up his hand. As his fingers unwound, I could see he was holding a big glob of shit. While I stood there, he mumbled and started to rub the shit all over his head. I backed away from the cell, concentrating on holding on to my lunch.

When I got to Pete's office, he poked me in the stomach and said, "Nice, huh!" That almost finished me. I asked, "That is Foxie in there, isn't it?" When he nodded I said, "You'd better fill me in." Pete said he didn't know what was happening for sure, but one of his snitches told him that Foxie was going to court tomorrow. Pete said, "It looks like Foxie is facing felony charges and a big sentence this time. My snitch thinks it's an act so he can cop a plea (i.e., plead insanity or get charged with a lesser offense)." I said, "No one is that desperate."

"We'll see," Pete said.

The next day, right after roll call, Pete called and said that there was someone who wanted to see me.

When I entered the office, there sat Pete and Foxie. Each had coffee and a cigarette. I did a double take.

Foxie was his old self. I couldn't resist saying, "Ah, the wonders of modern medicine. I'll put you in for the Nobel

Prize if you can tell me how you cured this asshole." Pete said, "It wasn't hard. All it took was the judge allowing him to cop to a misdemeanor. The judge should get the prize."

Foxie had a look of bewildered concern on his face. "Honest, Sarge, I don't remember a thing. Pete was just telling me what I did yesterday. It makes me sick! How could someone do that and not remember?" I looked in his eyes and knew he was trying to "blow smoke up my chimney." I said, "I don't think they can, but one thing is for sure." Foxie asked, "What's that, Sarge?" as he looked penitent. "From now on, when anyone calls you 'shithead', you can't argue about it." As Foxie's mouth popped open, I turned and left. Pete's laugh and "I told you so!" followed me out of the infirmary.

DB

DB are the initials for "Dough Boy," as in "Pillsbury Dough Boy." They were also the nickname of a corpulent black inmate that I met when I first started to work for the Department of Correction. DB was one of the inmates in a housing unit that I was assigned to supervise. I watched him one day as he left the shower room wearing his boxer shorts and shower clogs.

DB had no elbows or knees—just places where the fat kind of dimpled inward. His smiling, chubby face sat astride his slopping shoulders. He was about five feet, eight inches tall. But, it wasn't his size alone that impressed those that he met. DB's ever-present smile was as warm as it was genuine. He was never what you'd call jolly, but, rather, seemed happy to be alive.

DB was a burglar. That title didn't grant him a lofty position in the inmate pecking order. DB didn't seem to care about his social position. He made friends with all types of inmates except for the lower three—muggers, rapists, and child molesters. He knew that associating with those categories of inmates would only bring him trouble.

While we were at the Somers Prison, DB became interested in weightlifting and boxing. Almost overnight he seemed to have lost his happy-go-lucky air, and he became a COMPETITOR. He became intense, smiled less, and was always one of the first out of the cellblock when it came time for recreation in the gym. He stopped less at my desk to chat, and I wondered if the new mission in his life was worth losing the personality that I'd come to appreciate. Over several months of working out and being more selective in his diet, he shed over fifty pounds of baby fat, but his cherubic face remained the same.

One day I showed up to work his cellblock, and while taking a count, found that DB was gone. A check of the daily activities sheet showed that he'd been transferred to another institution. The next time I saw DB was at Seyms Street.

I was walking down a hallway when I noticed a newly admitted inmate coming toward me. His arms were overflowing with a blanket and sheets, and he was balancing a large paper bag on top of the other things.

The rolling gait seemed familiar, so I stopped and waited. As he approached, I said, "DB?" He peered from around the paper bag and said, "Oh, hi, Sarge!" He'd put back the weight he'd lost, but the smile and cheeriness were gone. He acted as though he'd seen me just yesterday. Preoccupation was carved in the lines that had formed in his face. After the usual, "How are you?" we went our own way. But something nagged at the back of my mind.

After my days off, I was touring the segregation unit in the Northwest Wing, and there was DB. "What are you doing here?" I asked. He mumbled, "Had some trouble." When I waited for an explanation, he said, "Never mind. No one can do anything." He rolled over and studied the wall, dismissing me.

When I looked into it, I found that he'd been in a fight. No one seemed to know what started it. I couldn't let it go. It was almost like finding out that one of the guys from the old neighborhood had died. You have to know why. I found the answer in his rap sheet. This part of an inmate's file lists all of his or her arrests in this state, and the disposition of each arrest. DB had had a string of burglary and larceny arrests which finally qualified him for graduation to the "big time"— a sentence in the state prison. His previous sentences sounded like a tour guide to penal institutions. He'd had a couple of probations (court supervision), a sentence to the youth institution at Cheshire, a few jail sentences, and Somers Prison. Unlike many of his peers, who showed progressing levels of violence in their crimes, DB had had no crimes involving injury to another—until now.

His rap sheet listed his latest arrest, rape, without going into further details.

Through the newspaper, I found that DB had been arrested for one of a series of rapes that the police thought were linked. He was being investigated for the others. The crimes involved brutal beatings to the victims. If he was guilty, something in DB had snapped. Something or someone had pushed the wrong button at the wrong time, and he'd exploded. That isn't to say that he wasn't responsible for the injury he had done, but to this day I wonder what was it that turned the Dough Boy into every woman's nightmare. I was soon to get a glimpse into his rage.

As I've previously stated, the Northwest Wing was in part used to house inmates who had violated the institution's rules. As you looked down the cell doors, on the upper levels (called "tiers") there was a five foot wide walkway, and then another set of bars that prevented anyone from falling (or being pushed) down to the ground level. The ends of the upper tiers had chain link gates that were locked whenever a segregation inmate was let out of his cell to shower. Each inmate was offered one hour for showering and recreation each day.

A few days after I'd checked DB's file, the call came: "All available officers to the Northwest Wing." The block officer was standing by the door when I arrived. "What's the problem?" I gasped. "DB, on the third tier broke up a chair and is threatening to kill anyone who tries to take it from him." I climbed the three flights and saw DB standing on the other side of the chain link gate. He was looking through the bars at the ground. "DB, what's the problem, man?"

DB turned at the sound of his name. He looked at me and, then, through me. His lips peeled back across his teeth as he bellowed, "No more! I ain't taking it no more!" As other staff arrived, I continued to try to talk to him. His eyes were a neon sign that flashed, "No one's home!" His face was covered in a sheen of sweat. The normal brown color had darkened to a near purple. He kept shouting, "No more! No more!" The pieces of a heavy wooden chair were strewn along the tier. DB's fingers were wrapped around the piece that had once formed the back and rear leg. It was three feet long and made of hardwood. Now, as he continued his chant, he began to keep time with himself by banging the chair leg against the shower stall.

I was standing close to the chain link gate as I tried to get him to talk. Finally, I decided to try one last thing, since I obviously was not getting through to him. I shouted, "SHUT THE FUCK UP!" And, he did! I went on in a lower tone, "DB, this is no good. You've got to tell me what's wrong." I thought for a second that I'd gotten to him. I thought that his mind was coming back from Never Never Land. Suddenly, he shouted and tried to hit me with the chair leg. Thank God for strong chain link fencing!

I backed off. He wasn't threatening anyone, and wasn't hurting himself. There was no need to rush into anything. After talking with Officer Billy Lynch, I agreed that he should give a try at talking to DB. That didn't work, either. When Billy returned to us downstairs, he said, "Sarge, we're going to have to take him."

As we talked, Officer Don Smith said, "Billy let's get a couple of mattresses. This was a new one to me. They explained that they intended to rush DB, using the mattresses as shields. I agreed that sounded like a good plan, and sent an officer for leg irons, handcuffs, and Mace. We decided that Billy and Smitty would go in shoulder to shoulder after I Maced DB. As they knocked him over, Officers Pat Butler and Eddie Colon would disarm him. The rest of us would get to him shortly after that and restrain him.

We lined up outside of the chain link gate. I said to DB, "Drop the chair and get back in your cell or I'm going to Mace you." He backed partway down the tier and took up a batter's stance. His "no mores" were reduced to a whisper as he became intent and focused. I Maced him. The gate flew open as the last droplets of tear gas reached him. Billy and Smitty charged. DB stood there, waiting, showing no effects from the Mace.

When they were four feet away, he brought the chair leg down across Smitty's mattress, almost dropping Smitty to the ground. They bowled him over and ran past him. As he tried to struggle to his feet, Pat hit him with a perfect body block to the shoulders. DB was swallowed in a sea of officers. Although he continued to struggle, we got the leg irons and handcuffs on him. As we brought him to his feet, I noticed that he was actually foaming at the mouth. The crazy thought went through my mind, "Gee that's neat! I've never seen anyone foam at the mouth before."

DB was taken to a mental institution the next day. I never saw him again.

Mr. Irreverent

Most of the correctional staff that I have worked with will go out of their way to be courteous to the public, their peers, and, most of all, their superiors. They do this despite the difficulty of their daily jobs.

An officer who was assigned to the Control Center at Seyms Street had so many tasks to perform that it always amazed me to hear one being polite on the telephone. An insensitive supervisor might pile additional tasks on an already overworked officer because that officer "got things done." An inmate might spit on an officer one day, and expect to be treated with respect the next. Through all of this, the officer was expected to maintain his or her equanimity, be amiable to giving and taking criticism, and never ever lose his or her temper. They were expected to be "professionals."

People (and despite what some would have you think, officers are people) handled the resultant stress in different ways. Some of their coping mechanisms were effective and some were disastrous to the careers and mental health of the folks who used them. There was one person at Seyms Street who had a unique way of dealing with the things that would make most of us withdraw and bottle up our hostilities. I think his outspoken irreverence often brought our egos down to earth, and we had to laugh at ourselves. Perhaps we were even refreshed by the experience. I'll call him Dominic Irreverante.

A typical example of Dom's irreverence occurred after Seyms Street had closed, and he was in another institution. A warden, who I'll call "John" was walking down a hallway in the opposite direction from Dom. As they approached, the warden, using his "noblesse" status by calling subordinates by their first names said, "How are you, Dom?" Dom replied, "Fine, John. How are you?" The warden, who probably sensed some irreverence that he feared might lead to insubordination, stopped Dom. He said, "Dom, I didn't know that we were on a first name basis." Dom thought about this a moment and said, "That's right, John. Neither did I!" Then he turned and continued on his way.

I was not immune from Dom's treatment. I was a brand-new sergeant, who was conscious that he had risen from the officer ranks. I was a plum ready for Dom's style of picking.

One night, he and I were attempting to subdue a particularly violent inmate. We weren't winning. A little voice in my head said, "Fuck this! You're going to get hurt!" So, I threw a punch at the inmate's head. As luck would have it, Dom's hand was holding the inmate's head, and I punched the back of his hand.

In those days, you never admitted to punching an inmate. That was not considered "reasonable force." Of course the department did not teach any form of self-defense, and when some poor newcomer asked an academy instructor, "What do

I do if I'm attacked?" the instructor would say, "Do what you have to!" Because we perceived that we would get no backing from the department in use of force situations, we tended to be a little creative in our report writing. Thus, my striking Dom's hand turned into his slamming it against a wall during the struggle. He and I knew different.

Since Dom was complaining of pain in his hand after the incident, I told him to go to the emergency ward. He returned to the institution with a report that said nothing was wrong with his hand, and he should just apply cold compresses until the swelling went down.

The next day before roll call, I asked Dom how his hand was doing. He flexed it gingerly and said, "It's still a little sore, but okay." When I went in to hold roll call, several officers were obviously biting their lips to hold back laughter. I read the notices for the day and started to give out post assignments. When I got to Dom's name, he shouted, "Here," at the top of his lungs. Everyone looked up and saw Dom holding up his "injured" hand. It was wrapped in bandages and looked like a boxing glove. The whole shift broke up. After the laughter died down, Dom said, "Hey, Sarge, can I have an easy duty post? You know, one where I won't have to respond to all available calls with you?"

We had an inmate who many considered a "bad ass." He was an enforcer for the Black Panthers, and a suspect in several murders. Although he was usually jovial, he had been known to lose his temper and display fierce violence. He was assigned to the kitchen.

Dom was the kitchen officer on this particular day. The inmate came in to the officers' mess to steal some food from our serving line, and Dom caught him. Dom called the seemingly penitent inmate to a table where four staff were sitting. He said, "You got any dough for cakes back there?" The inmate was eager to make amends for being caught. He said, "Sure, Mr. Irreverante. You want I should bake you a cake or something?" Dom thought a moment (while those of us who knew him held our breaths) and said, "No. I want you to go back in the kitchen and roll that dough out flat." The inmate adopted a position that showed that he was listening carefully to the instructions. "Can you do that?" Dom asked. "Yes sir!" The inmate thought a moment and asked, "But then what do I do with it?"

Dom stood up and walked to another table that was unoccupied. He said, "You've got all that dough rolled out, right?" The inmate nodded assent. "Now, starting at the upper left hand corner, I want you to do this."

Dom proceeded to bang his forehead against the table, going from left to right, and making several rows. The inmate looked at him like he was crazy, but he didn't want to show it because it could blow his chances to get back into Dom's good graces. He said, "Sir, why do you want me to do that?" Dom said, "Cause I want some gorilla cookies." The inmate tightened his grip on the tray he was holding and his jaw clenched. We were sure that Dom was going to wear that tray of half eaten food. After a second, the inmate visibly relaxed and said, "Ah, shit! Everyone knows that you're crazy!"

After work one night, Dom went to a Howard Johnson's with Larry Meyers and Pat Cammarato. After they'd had several drinks at the bar, Pat suggested that they go out front and have some coffee before driving home. They were all in uniform, although Dom and Larry partially concealed this fact by wearing civilian jackets.

As they walked through the aisle, they passed two "hip-pie" types who were sitting at a window seat. The hippies had long, unkempt hair and wore ripped clothes. They were also unacquainted with soap. Upon seeing Pat's uniform, one loudly stated, "Here come some of those asshole jail guards." Pat paused and steam started to come out of his ears. He was proud of his job and his uniform. The harangue continued, "They ain't shit without their clubs and Mace. All they know how to do is beat-up on people." Larry grabbed Pat's elbow and said, "Ignore those assholes."

The three of them sat at a nearby booth and ate their pie and coffee. While the officers tried to maintain their tempers, the hippies continued berating them. Unable to take it anymore, the three officers paid their bill and left, to the merriment of the hippies.

As they walked to the parking lot, Dom said, "Go back to your cars and leave your guns there. Then come back here." Knowing that he had something planned for their tormentors, they complied. Dom went to his trunk and took out his .357 magnum with a six inch barrel—an awesome looking cannon. He went up the walkway to the window that the hippies were seated at. After stepping over some shrubbery, he stood at their window and smiled. When they saw him standing there just smiling, they began to get nervous. At just the right moment, Dom brought the gun from behind his back and tapped on the window. Then he gestured to them to come on out and play.

Even through the window their screams of, "He's got a gun!" could be heard as one tried to crawl under the table while the other hit the floor in the aisle. As the manager came running over, Dom hid the gun under his coat. He stood outside the window, hands behind his back, smiling. During the chaos that was created in the restaurant, Dom walked back to his car while the manager called the police.

Seconds later eleven cruisers burned rubber as they squealed into the driveway. Dom had returned the weapon to his trunk. The three officers stood in the parking lot with a look of surprise on their faces. The manager and the two hippies flew out of the restaurant with their fingers pointing at Dom.

When everyone was calmed down, the sergeant in charge spoke to Dom (they knew each other from dealings at the jail). "What's going on?" Dom, indicating the two hippies, said, "Sarge, I know we were wrong, but those two were badmouthing us while we were drinking our coffee. They said a lot of shit like all of us 'fucking pigs' were the same and they'd like to see what would happen if we didn't have our guns. We didn't have any guns, but didn't want to start anything in the restaurant. They wouldn't come out when they saw us out here. I guess that's why they called you guys."

When Dom was informed that they were summoned because of a "man with a gun call," he acted amazed and offered himself to be searched. Because no firearms were found, and Dom kept suggesting that the rag-bags were bad-mouthing cops, too, they let the three officers go and spent more than a little time checking out the hippies. As the three parted, Dom said, "Ah, the power of the badge."

Dom's put-downs went across racial, social, and economic boundaries. It didn't matter *who* you were as much as *what* you were and *how you acted* that carried weight with him. One incident almost cost him his job.

It did not occur at Seyms Street but at the new jail that replaced Seyms Street.

Dom had drawn the outer lobby as his post. Part of his job was to maintain order in that area while signing up people who wanted to visit the inmates. Between answering the telephone and taking in bond money, this was a hectic post. As Dom was trying to do his job, a little black lady came to the window. After getting his attention she said, "Officer, I don't want to cause any trouble, but that lady over there isn't minding her children. One of them tripped over my foot. They're going to hurt someone or themselves. Can you do something about this?" He indicated that he would. After the elderly lady had resumed her seat he called out, "Whose kids are these?"

An obese black woman looked up from her knitting and said, "They're mine! What of it?" Dom explained that she would have to keep them quiet and stop them from running around. She said, "They're children. They have to play." Dom said, "Look lady, they can't play here. If you can't control them you'll have to leave." After a few "well I nevers" she called the brats to her and told them to sit down. They did—for about five seconds.

Dom answered the phone, did a few other tasks, and looked up as one of the kids crashed into a garbage can, sending its contents across the waiting room. Their keeper barely looked up and did not say anything to them. She looked at Dom as if to say, "I dare you to say something!"

Dom called her back to the window. When she had stuck her impatient ear next to the opening, he whispered in a soft voice, "Lady, if you don't control those kids, I'm going to wet their lips and stick them to the glass." She went through the roof! Of course no one could hear him so there were no witnesses when she complained to the governor.

"Our Fearful Trip Is Done"

The Seyms Street Jail was closed in July, 1977, after one hundred and four years of existence. After lengthy and sometimes difficult planning, inmates were shackled and put on buses. There was an air of expectation as each wondered about the new jail and how its conditions would impact their lives.

Supplies from Symms Street were shipped on trucks to the new institution. Even after all the inmates were in their new home, there were still crates of supplies and some personal property left.

Lieutenant Barton was assigned the job of disposing of the old personal property. These were items that had been confiscated from inmates who were being admitted to the jail.

They were suppose to leave with the inmate when he was transferred to another institution or released. Sometimes the inmates forgot to ask for the items when they left, or a harried staff member forgot to check to see if we were holding anything for a discharging inmate. The end result was that we had rooms full of these items that, by law, we couldn't throw out.

Jim had to copy the name and inmate number off of each bag or box, find the last known address from our records, and notify each person by registered mail that we were holding property that belonged to him. In some cases there weren't any names or numbers on the container. This forced him to go through the package to try to find that information. One day I went into the storage room and found Jim digging through such a box. He was surrounded by old, mildewed underwear and damp magazines. The smell in the room was really ripe.

I could see that he was frustrated by the way he was dumping the items out of the box. When he saw me he said, "This is ridiculous! I had a bag for a guy that had been locked up in 1970. I mailed him a letter that cost a buck to mail. The other day the guy calls me from Springfield (a toll call) to ask what was in the package. I wasn't in, so an officer took his number, and I called back (another toll call). The guy didn't think he'd left anything at Seyms Street. So I told him that I had a package for him somewhere in the store room. If he'd let me know when he'd be able to pick it up, I'd dig it out for him in advance. He agreed to drive down from Springfield the next day. When he got here, I gave him his bag.

"Add the costs up: a registered letter, two toll calls, and a round trip from Springfield. When he opened the package, do you know what was in it? Two old packs of cigarettes! When he took them out of the bag, I thought he was going to lose it. He stood there for a moment, took a deep breath, and as he threw the smokes on the floor and walked out he said, 'I quit smoking!'"

As he was telling me the story, I looked around the room. My eyes roamed over, and finally returned to, an artificial leg.

I stood gawking at it. How did someone leave the jail and forget their artificial leg? It's not like they wouldn't notice when they tried to walk down the steps. Certainly, no one has a spare that they carry around with them when they get arrested. The more I thought about it, the more I had to know. I asked Jim. He asked me to see if there was a name on it. I found the name and number and repeated them to him. He thought a moment and said, "Oh, yeah, I remember him. He escaped from the sheriffs a few years back." I almost screamed, "Escaped! without his leg?"

Curiosity now had me firmly in its teeth and was shaking the hell out of me. I wrote down the number and name and went to our records department. I pulled the inmate's information up on the computer screen. He had been recaptured and was still at the Somers Prison.

I knew some people at Somers, so I called a friend and explained the story. I asked him to check with the inmate and get back to me. A little while later I heard his chuckling voice returning my call.

I asked, "Did you talk to him? What did he say?" It seems that before the inmate escaped he had been fitted for a new prosthesis, but he left before it arrived. When it was delivered, no one knew what to do with it since the inmate hadn't been recaptured yet. It was dumped into storage. I told Jim the story and he had it shipped to Somers. He said, "Who cares if it still fits or not? Let them store it!"

After we moved out of Seyms Street, it was boarded up. Trucks still arrived during the day to take equipment and supplies out. Maintenance men scrounged through its halls looking for particular items that might be needed in the new jail. Some toilet bowls were removed and shipped. Some of the staff who got permission were allowed to go back in and take pictures.

One day we got a call from the Hartford Police who informed us that the old jail was being broken into. A party went over and found signs of entry. When they explored the inside they found crates of old-style officer uniforms opened. Further exploration uncovered some kids sleeping in the old cells. The cells had been left unlocked and these enterprising people had found some old mattresses. Someone suggested that we just lock the cells and let them see if they could break out as easily as they broke in. We ended up just shagging them out and reboarding it.

I remember thinking at the time that abandoning the old jail was like leaving a pine board lying in the grass. Eventually, the insects would begin eating into it and it would finally rot and crumble. That didn't seem like a fair ending for the old jail.

In the end, it wasn't the dignity of the old building that caused the "powers that be" to protect her for a while. They were more concerned with the legal liability issues involved. We were told to assign staff to act as watchmen until a better arrangement could be made. It was a spooky assignment, walking with the ghosts and Old Ben through the deserted halls. Was that noise just a rat or was someone trying to break in? Finally, a private security company took over the vigil until the jail was torn down.

Epilogue

I drove down North Main Street recently. I turned off by the old cemetery. The block was bordered by Seyms Street, Center Street, Mather Street, and East Street.

It was a foggy night, but I could make out parts of the little park that sits where the jail once was. The park seems too small to have held a building so large with memories.

I looked at the neighborhood with new eyes. It seemed as rundown as ever, but I had time to discover the newest layers of trash and decay. I had time to think.

I mentioned earlier that statistics show that the average age at death for someone who has spent twenty years in corrections is fifty-eight. But, I'll bet that the gatherers of those figures didn't find a lot of people in their seventies or eighties. The intensity with which the flame of a correctional employee's life burns is too great to be long-lived. The risks, the danger, and the stress they constantly experience take too great a tax from their allotted years.

In writing this, I wanted the average person to see a side of the law enforcement world that he or she may never even get a glimpse of in their lives. I wanted the people who lived it with me (or had similar journeys in different times or places) to remember. Most importantly, I don't want the people who worked there, or the place, to be forgotten.

As I restarted my truck, I thought about what Officer Ramon Martinez (now a deputy warden) recently said, "A good correction officer never loses his keys. I still have my keys to the Seyms Street Jail. In this case, I lost the building."

www.ingramcontent.com/pod-product-compliance
Lightning Source LLC
Chambersburg PA
CBHW061302280526
45784CB00002B/863